IRISH SURNAMES

IRISH SURNAMES

Padraic O'Farrell

Gill & Macmillan

To Dylan

Gill & Macmillan Ltd
Hume Avenue, Park West
Dublin 12
with associated companies throughout the world
www.gillmacmillan.ie

© *Padraic O'Farrell 2002*
0 7171 3338 9

Print origination by Carole Lynch
Printed by The Guernsey Press, Guernsey

This book is typeset in 10/15pt Adobe Garamond.

The paper used in this book is made from the wood pulp
of managed forests. For every tree felled, at least one tree is
planted, thereby renewing natural resources.

*A catalogue record is available for this book
from the British Library.*

1 3 5 4 2

CONTENTS

INTRODUCTION

Internet access has propelled towards chaos a subject that was already complex – Irish genealogy. Gaudy green graphics invite the surfer to find clans' roots, even though there never was a clan system in Ireland. Much of the information presented is from the shamrock and shillelagh school of misty melancholia and can be inaccurate.

The inaccuracy is at times understandable. Experts in the field have always disagreed, offering conflicting theories on origins and evolutions, even on translations and Anglicisms. Students of their work can become confused in a maelstrom of claim and counter-claim.

Traces of a methodology in hereditary surnames began appearing in Ireland as early as the tenth century. A district belonged to a tribe or sect, consisting of a number of families and their retainers, all having blood relationships with the head family of the chieftain. The district would carry the name of the sept or of an illustrious member or ancestor. Adding the prefix Ó (from), Mac (son [of]) or, later, Giolla or Maol (servant, devotee [of]) to a personal name, or that of a chieftain or saint, established a surname. The feminine Ní (or Nic before a vowel) in Irish was a subsequent grammatical device, while Mc and M' are abbreviations of Mac. Prefixes were added to nicknames and personal descriptions too. As time progressed, obsequious pandering to a foreign establishment led to their being discarded.

To complicate matters, surnames without prefixes existed and, in the nineteenth and twentieth centuries, families sometimes *added* prefixes to assume more 'Irishness'. The influence of the Gaelic League, the 1916 Rebellion and the subsequent War of Independence also encouraged reintroduction of the prefixes.

There are many other anomalies and difficulties in this subject that a small book cannot hope to discuss. I have attempted to overcome the problem by including a glossary of terms and abbreviations.

In the main text, I include over fifty of the most common surnames found in Ireland, irrespective of where they originated. For each surname I list, in alphabetical order, Irish translations, derivatives, varieties, synonyms, distortions, toponymics and corruptions. Those in italics fit one of these categories but, in addition, are principal surnames. Many of these appeared in government notes for guidance of Registration Officers, published in 1890.

I have offered a sample motto in most cases. Mottoes are not common to every bearer of a surname and the sample I give is simply one motto used by one branch of a sept that may not even be Irish. The motto can be a war cry or maxim and is normally written on a scroll placed beneath the family's coat of arms (war cries sometimes appear above). Mottoes appeared in the fourteenth century but did not become common until the seventeenth.

I then suggest origins and list some bearers of the surname, tossing in an occasional morsel of anecdote, folklore, ballad or rhyme. Here my choice is idiosyncratic – bizarre at times. Why worry? As Desmond Tutu said during the service to mark his retirement from the archbishopric of Cape Town in 1996: 'We do have these extraordinary names … When you see the sign "African Primates Meeting" you expect someone to produce bananas.'

———————

Footnote for the superstitious: Irish folklore ordains that bearers of most of the surnames listed in this book are 'followed by the banshee', i.e. the female spirit wails outdoors before a death in the family. Those who escape are: Boyle, Callaghan, Collins, Doherty, Donnelly, Fitzgerald, Fitzpatrick, Hughes, Kane, Mahony, Nolan, O'Connell, White and Wilson.

BOYLE
Boal, Bole, Ó Baoighill, O'Boyle

Motto: E duobus unum (One out of two)

From *baoghal*, meaning 'danger', or from an archaic Irish word, *baigel*, meaning 'possession of profitable pledges' (*geall*: pledge or promise)? Scholars argue. The Donegal sept was almost as prominent as the O'Donnells and the O'Dohertys. O'Boyle's Island near Portnoo, County Donegal, the village of Ballyweel (Baile Uí Bhaoighill) near Donegal town and Bohill in County Down incorporate the name. Many Boyles of English origin became influential too. Regarded as being red in the face, a Limerick latched on to this feature:

> The O'Boyles were a terrible race
> And never in good state of grace.
> Good folk they would addle
> With cheeks red as raddle –
> A big angry Boyle [boil] on the face.

Sir Walter Raleigh's County Waterford lands became part of the estate of the 'First Colonial Millionaire' Richard Boyle (1566–1643). An English settler, he could be termed an early speculator who became First Earl of Cork and practised nepotism in having his family placed in lucrative marital situations.

Richard's son Robert (1627–91) was a friend of Isaac Newton. Dubbed 'The Father of Chemistry', his influence on the science was likened to that of

Copernicus on cosmology. He invented a vacuum pump and used it to discover 'Boyle's Law'. At eleven years of age, already studying at Eton, he went on a grand tour of Europe. Outspoken for his time, he recorded meeting two friendly friars and resisting the 'preposterous courtship [of the] gowned sodomites'. An electric storm made him deeply religious. He became Provost of Eton.

Henry Boyle, Earl of Shannon (1682–1764), became Chancellor of the Exchequer, Commissioner of Revenue in Ireland and Speaker of the Irish House of Commons (1733–53).

Dublin-born engineer Richard Vicars Boyle (1822–1908) worked extensively on Irish, Indian and Japanese railways.

The town of Boyle took its name from its monastery (*Mainister na Búaille*).

More recently

In January 1970 Joseph Jablonski, a defeated reform candidate for President of the United Mine Workers' Union (UMW), his wife and daughters were found murdered in Clarksville, Pennsylvania. Four years later W.A. 'Tony' Boyle, UMW President, was convicted of ordering the assassination.

Better known than many modern bearers of the name is the fictitious Captain Jack Boyle, Sean O'Casey's malingering labourer in *Juno and the Paycock* (1924):

He's promised he'll come back to me
When the robins nest again.

BRADY

Briody, Mac Brádaigh, MacBrady

Motto: Vincit omnia virtus (Virtue conquers all)

Bradach means 'plunderer' and the verb is *bradaigh*, but *brod* or *broid* also means 'urging'. Brady was a powerful Breffny sept. A branch of the Dalcassian Ó Grádaigh (O'Grady) sept took the name during the sixteenth century and their descendants are still scattered across Counties Clare and Limerick. A descendant, Hugh Brady (whose father was O'Grady), was Bishop of Meath (1563–83).

Nicholas Brady (1659–1726) of Bandon, County Cork, became rector of Stratford-upon-Avon. With the Dublin-born Poet Laureate, Nahum Tate (1652–1715), he published a metrical edition of the Psalms. He also translated Virgil's *Aeneid*.

The anonymous song about the Bold Phelim Brady, a 'poor Irish harper', is often regarded as a cryptic reference to St Oliver Plunkett's undercover administration of his Armagh archbishopric:

> It was long 'fore the shamrock, our green isle's
>   loved emblem
> Was crushed in its beauty 'neath Saxon's lion's
>   paw,
> I was called by the colleens of village and valley,
> The Bold Phelim Brady, the Bard of Armagh.

Irish convicts in west Australia found an ally in its Vicar General, Rev. John Brady. He also had regard for aborigine tribes. A native of Cavan, he had laboured for twelve years in Mauritius, before going to Australia in February 1838.

'Diamond Jim' (James Buchanan) Brady (1856–1917) amassed a fortune by pioneering railroads and their equipment. Allegedly, he was the son of an Irish gypsy. A former bellboy, he collected thirty complete sets of jewellery valued at well over a million dollars. His enormous appetite made him a celebrity in Broadway social life. In 1912 he financed the James Buchanan Brady Urological Institute at Johns Hopkins Hospital, Baltimore.

More recently

'Brady's Clock' in a porter keg over a public house has been showing the time to travellers through Maynooth since at least the 1930s.

'Gunner Brady' was a worshipped Cavan footballer while Liam Brady was an equally lauded Irish soccer international.

BRENNAN

Branan, Braniff, Brannan, Brannen, Brannie, Brannon, Branon, Breanon, Brenan, Brennen, Brennon, Brenon, Brinane, Mac Branáin, MacBrennan, Ó Braonáin, O'Brennan

Motto: Si Deus nobiscum, quis contra nos? (If God be with us, who can be against us?)

The simple translation of *braon* is 'drop' while

braonach is 'dripping', 'misty' or 'wet'. *Bréan* is 'foul' or 'evil' and *brón* is 'sorrow'. None of these can be established satisfactorily as the origin of Brennan. The two Gaelic forms above were once used for five septs of which one was Mac Branáin and the other four were Ó Braonáin. Eventually all were Anglicised to Brennan. The main sept was in Ossory, but others were prominent in Counties Roscommon, Mayo, Galway, Westmeath, Kerry and Sligo.

Recalled by the ballad-singing Clancy Brothers, 'Captain' William Brennan was a popular outlaw who, armed with a blunderbuss, operated in Cork's Kilworth Mountains during the eighteenth and nineteenth centuries. He was captured and executed in Clonmel Gaol in 1840.

> Brennan on the Moor, Brennan on the Moor,
> Bold, brave and undaunted was young Brennan
> on the Moor.

Michael J. Brenan (1829–57) assisted John Mitchel in publishing the *United Irishman*. Later, he edited the *Irish Felon*. After emigrating to the US, he became editor of the *New Orleans Times*.

Robert Brennan (1881–1964) led the 1916 Rebellion in Wexford and was Director of Elections in 1918 for Sinn Féin's sweeping seventy-three-seat victory. He was Under Secretary and main organiser of the underground Department of External Affairs during the Irish War of Independence and then opposed the Treaty. He became the first general manager of the *Irish Press*, Minister Plenipotentiary in Washington and Director of Broadcasting in Radio Éireann.

William J. Brennan-Whitmore (1886–1977) was a revolutionary and journalist. An intelligence officer for Michael Collins, he outlived all other 1916 leaders and was the most senior ranking Volunteer to leave a memoir (*Dublin Burning: The Easter Rising from behind the Barricades*, 1996). He edited a County Wexford newspaper, *The Record*.

More recently

Clare man Michael Brennan was an Irish War of Independence and Irish Civil War leader who, with the rank of Major General, became Chief of Staff of the Irish army (1931–40).

BURKE
Bourke, de Búrca, de Burg(h), de Burg(o)

Motto: Ung roy, ung foy, ung loy (One king, one faith, one law)

The most numerous and most eminent Hiberno-Norman name is found all over Ireland, having spread from a Connaught base. Burke is the normal spelling for the Upper (Galway) branch and Bourke for the Lower (Mayo).

During the Anglo-Norman invasion, William de Burgo introduced the name. Between 1180 and 1272, de Burgos received large territories from two kings. Although the writ of the Tribes of Galway denied them entry to the city, they above all invaders 'became more Irish than the Irish themselves'.

MacWilliams, MacDavies, Mac Seóiníns, McRedmonds, Jennings and Gibbons evolved from Burke influences here and in Scotland and Wales.

The sixteenth-century pirate queen Granuaile (Grace O'Malley) took Richard, chief of the Mayo Bourkes, as her second husband. Their son, Tibbot na Long (1567–1629; *long*: ship), defected to the English during the Battle of Kinsale and was rewarded handsomely with extensive properties. In 1508 and in 1580, de Burgos were bishops in Clonfert but by that time the form 'Burke' was firmly established.

Dublin-born Edmund Burke (1729–97) was a statesman, writer and Whig orator of note. He broke with his party by denouncing the French Revolution. A county in Georgia, USA, is called after him.

Genealogist John Burke (1787–1848) published *Burke's Peerage* and *Burke's Landed Gentry*.

William Burke (1792–1829) was hanged in Edinburgh for selling cadavers for dissection, having strangled most of them himself. From this emanated the intransitive verb 'burke'. His partner was William Hare and they sold to a Dr Knox. A children's street rhyme went:

Burke's the murderer, Hare's the thief
And Knox the boy who buys the beef.

The motto above belonged to the Clanricarde earls, of whom Ulick was the first. The Second Marquess and Fifteenth Earl of Clanricarde, Hubert George de Burgo Canning (1832–1916), MP for County Galway, was a despised absentee landlord who ordered evictions and refused tenants permission to purchase their holdings at Woodfield, Portumna.

More recently

Margaret Burke-Sheridan (1889–1958) was a celebrated soprano.

Dublin's Bourkes were involved in theatre production, costuming, lighting and history. Their Abbey Street premises served as the first RTÉ studio.

BYRNE

Beirne, Berne, Bierne, Birne, Birnes, Bourn, Bourne, Burn, Burnes, Burns, *Byrnes*, Byrns, *Byron*, McBrin, Mucbrin, O'Beirne, Ó Broin, O'Byrne

Motto: Shillelagh Abú (Shillelagh [in County Wicklow] forever)

The Irish word *bran* can mean 'raven', 'bream' or 'bran' and Bran was a mid-eleventh-century King of Leinster. Genealogists, however, opt for 'raven' as the origin for Byrne. Burns is sometimes a corruption but mainly it is a Scottish surname in its own right.

'Throw a stone in County Wicklow and you'll

hit a Byrne', people said long before Irish television soaps *Bracken* and *Glenroe* bestowed the name on their sheep-farmers. Yet the sept lived mainly in territory that is now, substantially, County Kildare. The Anglo-Norman invasion forced them and the O'Tooles to retreat to the Wicklow Mountains. The O'Byrnes chose the southern chain. While elders dissipated, a junior branch survived along the Avoca River and westward across the hills to the County Carlow border. Fierce in their resistance to Crown forces, their headquarters was on Ballinacor Mountain. Enemies entered *Crioc Branach* (O'Byrne territory) with trepidation.

When Fiach MacHugh O'Byrne (*c.* 1544–97) was chieftain he became a thorn in the side of the Establishment through his frequent sorties from Ballinacor on targets within the Pale. He won a major victory in 1580. In the same year, to avenge the murder of a kinsman, he attacked and ravaged lands in County Wexford.

He received several pardons but had a habit of lying low for a while, then going on the rampage again. Lord Deputies became frustrated, especially Sir William FitzWilliam. There was then a price on Fiach's head.

Routed from Ballinacor once, he teamed up with the Earl of Tyrone, Hugh O'Neill, to recover it. Eventually a force under Sir William Russell captured and beheaded Fiach. That was in May 1597.

Fiach and many other Byrnes and O'Byrnes are remembered in the 'Book of the O'Byrnes' (*Leabhar Branach*; see Fitzpatrick, Brian). In the stirring 'Marching Song of Fiach MacHugh', better known as 'Follow Me Down to Carlow', the poet P.J. McCall wrote:

> Curse and swear, Lord Kildare!
> Fiach will do what Fiach will dare –
> Now FitzWilliam, have a care;
> Fallen is your star low!
> Up with halberd, out with sword,
> On we go for, by the Lord,
> Fiach MacHugh has given his word:
> 'Follow me down to Carlow.'

Miles Byrne (1780–1862) participated in the 1798 Rebellion in Wexford and fought at Vinegar Hill. He marched north and joined with Michael Dwyer to hold out long after the fight had ended in other areas. The patriot Robert Emmet then sent him to France to persuade Napoleon to send an expeditionary force to assist another Irish rebellion. An Irish Legion emerged and Byrne distinguished himself as one of its officers, becoming a Knight of the Legion of Honour (*Chevalier de Légion d'Honneur*). Not on Ireland's behalf, however, but Napoleon's – in the campaigns of 1804–15.

Bishop Andrew Byrne (1802–62) was a pioneer of Roman Catholicism among the American Indians.

Three Byrnes – Ben, Eddie and Vincent – were

members of Michael Collins's squad known as the 'Twelve Apostles' while Charlie Byrne was in his intelligence section.

More recently

One of the most popular men bearing the name was Alfie Byrne (1882–1956), who had been elected Lord Mayor of Dublin ten times when he received an honorary Doctorate of Law from Dublin University in 1955.

Tony Award winner Jack Keyes Byrne is better known as playwright Hugh Leonard.

Gay Byrne hosted RTÉ's record-breaking television chat show, *The Late Late Show*, for thirty-seven years (1962–99). His radio programme, *The Gay Byrne Show*, ran for twenty-six years (1972–98).

CALLAGHAN

Calaghan, Calahan, Callaghen, Callagher, Callaghin, Callahan, Callaughan, Calleghan, Callehan, Calligan, Callighan, Kelaghan, Kellaghan, Kelleghan, *O'Callaghan*, Ó Ceallacháin

Motto: Fidus et audax (Faithful and bold)

Ceallach means 'recluse' or 'hermit' but 'strife' has also been suggested as a translation. The tenth-century Munster king, Ceallacháin, was the eponymous ancestor. Cromwell forced them from their County Cork lands to County Clare, as the village of O'Callaghan's Mills near Tulla and the

O'Callaghan Westropp family bear witness. The name sometimes evolved as a corruption of Kelleghan or O'Kelaghan, an Oriel sept that settled in the midlands, particularly in County Westmeath, where a 'Book of the Kelleghans' existed until recently. Similarly, Kelleghan sometimes became Callaghan.

In June 1887, a crowd of 5,000 gathered to witness the eviction of twenty-eight families from the Bodyke, County Clare, estate of Colonel John O'Callaghan.

Dubliner John Cornelius O'Callaghan (1805–83) was on the editorial staff of *The Nation*. He spent a quarter of a century researching his *History of the Irish Brigades in the Service of France* (1870).

Colonel George O'Callaghan Westropp (1864–1944) was aide-de-camp to three British kings and later an Irish senator and farmers' leader.

More recently

Pat O'Callaghan (1905–91) was the first athlete from an independent Ireland to have the tricolour raised at an Olympic Games. He won the hammer event in Amsterdam in 1928. He won another gold medal in 1932 at Los Angeles and set an unofficial world record of 195 feet 4 $^7/_8$ inches at Fermoy, County Cork, in 1937.

James Callaghan, British Home Secretary, visited the Bogside in Derry during its troubled August of 1969. He was later Prime Minister (1976–79).

CARROLL

Cardwell, Caroll, Carrolly, *MacCarroll*, McCarvill, Mac Cearbhaill, O'Carroll, Ó Cearbhaill

Motto: In fide officioque fortis (Strong in faith and duty)

Literally, the Irish *cearbhail* means 'grumbling', but the name presents difficulties because there were two distinct septs of Mac Cearbhaill and many of the distinctly divorced Ó Cearbhaill. Of the latter, the Ely and Oriel Ó Cearbhaills were of particular significance.

Cearbhal, the Lord of Ely who fought at the Battle of Clontarf (1014), was a descendant of the third-century King of Munster, Oilioll Olum. The Norman Butlers forced the sept off their vast lands in Munster and they settled mainly in County Offaly.

A contributor to the Book of Armagh, Maolsutháin Ó Cearbhaill, was confessor to Brian Boru.

In his *Chronicum Scotorum: A Chronicle of Irish Affairs from the Earliest Times to 1135*, Dubhaltach Mac Firbisigh (*c.* 1600–71) wrote in praise of Offaly's bountiful Margaret O'Carroll. The daughter of Thady O'Carroll, King of Ely, was, he said, 'a woman that never refused any man in the world for anything that she might command, except her own body'. In verse, Thomas D'Arcy McGee (1825–68) lauded her too:

But the name of Margaret Carroll, who taught
    the might of love,
Shall shine in Ireland's annals even minstrels'
    names above.

A Jesuit, John Carroll (1735–1815) was
America's first Roman Catholic bishop and
Baltimore's first archbishop. A friend of statesman
Benjamin Franklin, he supported the patriot cause
against Britain in the American Revolution and
secured toleration of Roman Catholicism.

Charles Carroll (1737–1832) was a signatory of
the American Declaration of Independence.

Charles Lutwidge Dodgson (1832–98) was
better known by his pseudonym Lewis Carroll. He
wrote *Alice's Adventures in Wonderland* and *Through
the Looking Glass*.

More recently

From Dundalk, County Louth, came P.J. Carroll
who established a leading tobacco company. At
Blackrock, near the same town, playwright Paul
Vincent Carroll (1900–68) was born. Two of his
plays – *Shadow and Substance* and *The White Steed* –
won the New York Drama Critics' Circle Award for
best foreign play.

In October 1980, Mella Carroll became
Ireland's first female High Court Judge.

Brendan O'Carroll is a successful comedian,
writer and businessman and Johnny Carroll a
popular trumpeter.

CLARK/CLERY
Clairke, Clarke, Cleary, Clerk, Clerkin, Clery, O'Cleary, Ó Cléirigh, O'Clery

Motto: Carpe Diem (Seize the present opportunity)

Both surnames come from the Irish form, Ó Cléirigh. *Cléirach* means 'clerk' but Ó Cléirigh was an early hereditary surname in County Galway and Cleireach was of the Guaire line (see below). Early in the fourteenth century, the name spread and a literary sept emerged in County Donegal. In parts of Desmond and Leinster and in Breffny, Anglicisation produced Clark and Clarke in some cases, Clery and its variants in others. Clearys claim descent from the sixth-century Connaught king, Guaire Aidhnach, 'Guaire the Hospitable', whose castle (later rebuilt) near Kinvara is now a medieval banqueting location.

Folklore tells of Guaire participating in a lavish Easter banquet. Seven miles away, at Kilmacduagh, St Colmán Mac Duagh and his Mass server were starving in their hermitage. The food being served to Guaire and his guests miraculously became airborne. Diners followed the speeding salvers and all touched down at Colmán's hermitage. The 'tracks' of the retinue survived as *Bóthar na Mias*, 'The Road of the Dishes'.

Donegal-born Micheál Ó Cléirigh (*c.* 1575–1643), 'Tadhg of the Mountains', has been credited with rescuing Ireland's past, while serving as a Franciscan brother at Louvain. He, his cousin Cúchoigcríche Ó Cléirigh and two others were the 'Four Masters' who compiled the Annals of the Kingdom of Ireland.

Desirée and Julie Cleary had an Irish father. Under Napoleon, they became, respectively, queens of Sweden and Spain.

Thomas Clarke (1857–1916) was the first signatory of the Proclamation of the Irish Republic. He spent four years planning the 1916 Rebellion and was executed for his participation in it. His wife Kathleen (1878–1972) was a revolutionary and member of Cumann na mBan.

More recently

An illustrator, designer and lecturer, Harry Clarke (1889–1931) excelled in stained glass.

University College Dublin lecturer Austin Clarke (1896–1974) won awards for his poetry, some of which he printed on his own hand press.

And if we wish to enter the domain of personal names, Clark Gable (1901–60) didn't give a damn!

COLLINS
Colins, *Culhane*, Cullane, *Cullen*, Cullian, McCallan, Mac Coileáin, Ó Coileáin, O'Cullane

Motto: Fide et virtute (By faith and valour)

While *coileán* means 'pup' or 'cub', in personal

application it can suggest 'scion', 'youth', 'fighting man' or even 'trickster'. None may be relevant, however, because although regarded now as an indigenous Irish name, Collins was always common in England. The Irish surname is most prevalent in Counties Cork and Kerry. Cullane was a County Limerick sept while Mac Coileáin flourished mainly in Ulster.

The Geraldines drove early Desmond septs southward from their Upper Connello lands and at the end of the thirteenth century they were found mainly in west Cork. The deprivation was evoked in the poem 'Machtnamh an Duine Dhoilghíosaigh' ('The Meditation of the Sorrowful One'). Despite some doubts, most scholars agree that a bitter, drinking schoolmaster, Seán Ó Coileáin (1754–1817), wrote it. It compares with Thomas Gray's (1716–71) 'An Elegy Written in a Country Churchyard', which may have served as a template for Ó Coileáin. This man banished his first wife and her sister whom he also married yet became known as 'The Silver Tongue of Munster'.

Sam Collins (1826–65), chimney sweep, was probably the first Irish comedian 'on the halls' in England. With billycock hat, shamrock and shillelagh, he popularised 'The Limerick Races', 'Paddy's Wedding' and 'The Rocky Road to Dublin'. In 1863, he opened Collins's Music Hall in Islington Green, London.

Michael Collins (1890–1922) fought in the

1916 Rebellion and led the guerrilla campaign during the Irish War of Independence. A Treaty plenipotentiary, during the Irish Civil War following its endorsement he was shot dead at Béal na mBláth, County Cork, on 22 August 1922.

County Cork born Patrick A. Collins was a popular Mayor of Boston (1902–05). An estimated 100,000 citizens turned out for his funeral.

More recently

Civil servant Thomas J. Collins (1894–1972) was co-editor with C.E. Kelly of *Dublin Opinion* from 1926 to 1968. With An tAthair Aindrias Mac Aogáin, he wrote two operettas, *Trághadh na Taoide* (*The Turning of the Tide*) and *Nocturne sa Chearnóg* (*Nocturne in the Square*).

Astronaut Michael Collins was a crew member when Apollo XI made its first manned lunar flight in July 1969.

CONNOLLY

Conally, Conelly, *Conlan*, Conley, Conlon, Conly, Connally, Connaly, Conneally, Conneelly, *Connell*, *Connellan*, Connelly, Connely, Connoly, Conolly, Conoly, Cunneely, McIneely, Ó Conghaile, Ó Congheallaigh, O'Connolly

Motto: En Dieu est tout (Everything is in God)

No connection with Conneely, two Gaelic Ó Conghaile septs had territories in Uí Máine and in Munster, while another shared properties in Galway and Monaghan. They adopted variations on the Gaelic form but, gradually, conformity evolved until Connolly is now almost universal.

William 'Speaker' Conolly (1662–1729) of Castletown House, Celbridge, County Kildare, features in folklore. He descended from the Munster sept. Out hunting with the 'Killing Kildares', William found a mysterious rider challenging his every feat. Fond of a spirited rival, he invited the dark stranger back to his splendid mansion for dinner, port and heated argument on politics of the day. During a card game afterwards, the battle of wits continued. At one stage, Conolly dropped a knave of clubs and stooped to retrieve it. He then saw his guest's cloven foot. Exposed, the Devil began causing havoc until a chambermaid ran to seek the services of the local curate. He came and a spiritual struggle ensued before Old Nick disappeared up the chimney in a puff of foul smoke. Conolly's home is now headquarters of the Irish Georgian Society.

Cork man Richard B. Connolly exaggerated his great height by wearing a stove-pipe hat when he worked his way up in New York banking to become the financial wizard of the infamous Tammany Hall 'Tweed Ring'. Called 'Slippery Dick', he became Comptroller at City Hall, exacerbating the corruption in municipal affairs that was rampant. Eventually cornered by reformers, he fled the US in 1873.

James Connolly (1868–1916) and his son
Roddy (1901–80) fought in the 1916 Rebellion.
Scottish, of Irish parents, James became an
organiser of socialism in Dublin and founded *The
Workers' Republic*. A signatory of the Proclamation
of the Irish Republic, he was executed on 12 May
1916. Roddy joined the first Communist Party in
Ireland and edited its journal. Later he served in
Dáil Éireann as a Labour TD. He was also a
senator and Chairman of the Labour Party.

Daughter of James (above), Nora Connolly
O'Brien (1893–1981) helped bring Liam Mellows
from England to attempt an uprising in Galway in
1916. During the Irish Civil War, she established
medical aid posts in Dublin and replaced Margaret
Skinnider as Austin Stack's assistant.

More recently

The first Irish detachment that joined the
International Brigade fighting against General
Franco in the Spanish Civil War (1936–39) chose
the title 'James Connolly Unit', better known as
the 'Connolly Column'.

Welsh-born Sybil Veronica Connolly
(1921–98) was one of Ireland's earliest and most
esteemed dress designers who made Irish lace
popular. Woman of the Year in Britain in 1958, she
was voted among the ten best-dressed women in
the world in 1957, 1958 and 1959 and ranked
among the ten leading designers in the world in
1960, 1961 and 1962.

'Little Mo', Maureen Connolly (1934–69) brought fashion to Wimledon and became one of America's most popular tennis champions. She won both the US and Wimbledon titles on three occasions.

DALY
Daily, Daley, Dawley, Dawly, Dayley, Dealy, Deely, Ó Dálaigh, O'Daly

Motto: Deo et regis fidelis (Faithful to God and king)

Dálach is a 'day of assembly' but *dalaigh* or *dáil* can mean 'assembly' or even a 'tryst'! A southern Uí Néill sept bearing the name occupied the County Westmeath barony of Magheradernan (later Molyngar, then Mullingar). Curonnacht Ó Dálaigh in neighbouring Meath was earliest in a line of literary Dalys. He supervised a bardic colony. The thirteenth-century Donough Mór Ó Dálaigh from County Clare was known as the 'Irish Ovid'. Carbery's Diarmaid Óg was poet of the Mac Cárthaighs but later Angus pilloried the Irish in his work *The Tribes of Ireland*. In Cavan and in Galway, O'Dalys and Dalys became influential during the eighteenth and nineteenth centuries.

Folklore tells how the romantic poet Cearbhall Ó Dálaigh (1590–1630) from County Wexford received his poetic skill from milking a magic cow.

Some claim that the term 'blackballing'

originated in Daly's Club, Dublin, meeting place for the infamous 'Hellfire Club'. Acceptance was decided by dipping into a bag. Picking a white ball allowed membership but black barred it. Actor and theatre proprietor Richard Daly (1750–1813) owned the club as well as Smock Alley, Crow Street and the Theatre Royal. 'The most opulent club in Europe' had its own way of dealing with card cheats. They were thrown from the upper-storey window on to the pavement below.

Edward Daly (1891–1916), a brother-in-law of Proclamation signatory Thomas Clarke, commanded a garrison at the Four Courts during the 1916 Rebellion. He was executed in Kilmainham Jail on 4 May.

Hearing of Black and Tan atrocities at home, Private James Daly of Tyrrellspass, County Westmeath, led a mutiny among the Connaught Rangers at Jullundur in the Punjab, India, in June 1920. He was executed.

Paddy Daly was second-in-command and sometimes leader of Michael Collins's 'Twelve Apostles'.

More recently

Cearbhall Ó Dálaigh (1911–78) became Attorney General, judge of the Supreme Court, Chief Justice, member of the Court of Justice of the European Communities and, by consensus, President of Ireland (December 1974). In October 1976 he interpreted a remark of the Minister for

Defence, Patrick Donegan, as an insult to his office and resigned.

Richard J. Daley (1902–76) was a celebrated Mayor of Chicago.

Cardinal Cahal Brendan Daly was Archbishop of Armagh and Primate of All Ireland. He has published papers, pamphlets and books, including *The Price of Peace* (1991) and *Steps on my Pilgrim Journey* (1998).

Then there's the lady famous for her mountain dew, invited in song to 'Come down from the mountain, Katie Daly'.

DOHERTY
**Daugherty, Dogherty, Dohorty, Dooherty,
Doorty, Dorrity, Dougherty, Ó Dochartaigh,
O'Doherty, O'Dougherty, Ó Dubhartaigh**

Motto: Ár nDúthchas (Our Heritage)

Dochrach means 'harmful', 'hurtful' or 'baleful' and the leading Doherty sept of Raphoe, County Donegal, may have displayed all three characteristics in extending their territories northward to include the complete Inishowen peninsula. A presence in Derry stems from survivors of an unwise attempt to annex lands there by Sir Cahir O'Doherty (1587–1608). This Lord of Inishowen had been knighted by Lord Mountjoy and was popular with Queen Elizabeth I. He captured and burned Derry in April 1608 and killed its Governor, Sir George Paulet, with whom he had had an earlier altercation. In July, he was proclaimed a traitor, and was shot and beheaded on 'The Rock of Doon' back in County Donegal. His recklessness prompted a decision to advance the Plantation of Ulster with Scottish settlers. Many of the O'Doherty chieftains fled to Spain.

The O'Donnells were closely connected and both septs claim Niall of the Nine Hostages as progenitor. The less common forms of the name (above) were associated mainly with Munster, particularly with County Clare.

Dublin Young Irelander Kevin Izod O'Doherty (1823–1905) was serving ten years' transportation in Tasmania (Van Diemen's Land) but received a pardon. After coming home, he studied medicine and made two trips to Australia. He had the distinction of being a member of Queensland Legislative Assembly (1877–85) and MP for County Meath (1885–88). His wife (née Mary Eva Kelly) was 'Eva of *The Nation*'.

Joseph O'Doherty from Derry was a member of the executive that planned the 1916 Rebellion. He organised volunteers in his home city at the behest of Seán MacDermott. He was TD for North Donegal in the First Dáil.

More recently

In August 1981, Kieran Doherty, TD for Cavan–Monaghan, died after a seventy-three day hunger strike at the Maze Prison, Belfast.

Jim Doherty is a popular Dublin jazz pianist.

Moya Doherty and John McColgan brought their initial concept for a Eurovision Song Contest interval act to the world-acclaimed *Riverdance* phenomenon.

DONNELLY

Dannelly, Donelly, Donely, *Donlan*, Donly, Donnally, *Donnell*, Donnely, Donnolly, O'Donnelly, Ó Donnghaile

No motto

Donn means 'brown' and *gal* can mean 'ardour', 'fury' and normally, in surnames, 'valour' (see O'Farrell). Donnghaile O'Neill of Cenél Eoghan was the eponymous ancestor of the Donnellys. Donnell O'Donnelly died fighting with Hugh O'Neill at the Battle of Kinsale (1601). The O'Donnellys moved to Castlecaulfield, near Dungannon, County Tyrone, giving it its former name, Ballydonnelly. Patrick O'Donnelly burned its castle in 1642. The Caulfields rebuilt it and allowed Oliver Plunkett to ordain priests within its courtyard. Meanwhile the O'Donnellys moved to County Antrim.

The name became significant in the USA, in law reform (Charles F., 1836–1909) and literature (Eleanor, 1838–1917).

Donnelly's Hollow on the plains of the Curragh was the arena for a celebrated bare-fisted fight.

Sensationally, Ireland's Dan Donnelly (1770–1820) beat England's George Cooper there in 1815.

> When Donnelly and Cooper had stepped into
>   the ring,
> 'Shake hands,' says Dan to Cooper, 'before we
>   do begin.'
> From six to nine they parried on, till Donnelly
>   knocked him down;
> Old Grania [Granuaile: Ireland] cried 'Well
>   done, my child! That's worth ten thousand
>   pound.'

Ignatius Donnelly (1831–1901), Lieutenant Governor of Minnesota, published an allegation that Francis Bacon wrote the plays attributed to William Shakespeare.

More recently

Charles Donnelly (1910–37) formed a left-wing group, Student Vanguard, in University College Dublin. He fought with the International Brigade (Abraham Lincoln Battalion) in the Spanish Civil War and was killed at Jarama. The military historian Sir Basil Liddell Hart (1895–1970) was impressed with Donnelly's theses on military strategy.

DONOVAN
Dingavin, Ó Donnabháin, *O'Donovan*

Motto: Adjuvante Deo in hostes (God assisting against enemies)

Céad Míle Fáilte, they'll give you down at
   Donovans;
Cheery as the springtime and Irish as the
   ceannabhán [bog cotton].

Donn is 'brown' and *bán* is 'white', so the fairish-brown 'mousy' hair colouring might be suspected here. However, most commentators agree an origin in the personal name Donnabhán (also Donndubán or Donnubán). Ninth- and tenth-century Munster chiefs of dark brown and swarthy appearance used it, *dubhán* being a derivative of *dubh*, meaning 'black'.

County Limerick via County Cork to County Kilkenny – that was the movement of the early O'Donovans. Once powerful, their influence diminished because of their close association with the Roman Catholic cause of King James II as 'O'Donovan's Infantry'.

In foreign armies, Donovans were prominent too and Dubliner Edmund O'Donovan (1844–83) was a member of the French Foreign Legion and a prominent war correspondent for *The Times* and other newspapers. Historians are indebted to his father, Kilkenny-born Dr John O'Donovan (1809–61), a pioneer of Celtic studies and translator of the Annals of the Kingdom of Ireland, whose 'Ordnance Survey Letters' form invaluable source material for researchers of place-names and social history.

It was Padraic Pearse's oration at the grave of

the dead Fenian Jeremiah O'Donovan Rossa
(1831–1915) that fomented belligerent
nationalism, particularly the statement 'They think
that they have foreseen everything, think that they
have provided against everything; but the fools, the
fools, the fools! – they have left us our Fenian dead
and while Ireland holds these graves, Ireland unfree
will never be at peace.'

Gerald O'Donovan (1871–1942) left the
priesthood to become a novelist. His
autobiography, *Father Ralph* (1915), was unusual
for the period in its anti-clerical innuendo.

More recently

Morgan Gerald Daniel O'Donovan, The
O'Donovan, son of Brigadier The O'Donovan MC
and Madam O'Donovan of Skibbereen, County
Cork, has been the formally recognised Chief of
the Name since his succession in 1969. His son
Morgan Tiege Gerald is Deputy Chief, or Tánaiste.

Actor Harry O'Donovan (1896–1973) travelled
Ireland with a 'fit-up' theatre company. He wrote
scripts for Jimmy O'Dea, with whom he formed
O'Dea–O'Donovan Productions. The partnership
created the ubiquitous 'Biddy Mulligan, the Pride
of the Coombe'.

In the 1960s, Donovan began a career that
made him the heartthrob of pop enthusiasts for his
'Mellow Yellow', 'Colours' and other numbers.

DOYLE
Doil, Dyle, MacDowell, McDowell, Mac Dubhghaill, MacDugall, O'Doyle, Ó Dubhghaill

Motto: Fortitudine vincit (He conquers by fortitude)

Before the Anglo-Norman invasion, the Irish *dubh gall*, or 'black foreigner', was frequently accorded to Norsemen. This is important in establishing the Norse origin of Doyle and its predating the Anglo-Norman invasion. Because of the similarity in structure, the Scotch settlers in County Roscommon (Lismacdowell), MacDugalls, who adopted the Irish spelling, are included here.

The name is found mainly in south-east Leinster. From the seventeenth century, it appears among high-ranking officers in British and Continental armies.

A celebrated writer and Bishop of Kildare and Leighlin, James Warren Doyle (1786–1834), spoke to parliamentary committees on the Irish situation and in urging a Poor Law. A diocesan disciplinarian, he became widely known for his pen-name, 'JKL'.

Sir Arthur Conan Doyle (1859–1930) who created Sherlock Holmes had Irish origins.

Painter Henry Edward Doyle (1827–92) was Commissioner for Rome in the 1862 London International Exhibition. A Knight of the Order of Pope Pius X, he became Director of the National

Gallery of Ireland in 1869 and acquired valuable works for exhibition during his twenty-three years' tenure.

'Linseed Oil' was more than a useful paint mix, cattle-feed additive or laxative. It became the popular soubriquet for Lynn C. Doyle, which was in turn the pen-name of County Down-born author Leslie Montgomery (1873–1961).

More recently

Jack Doyle (1913–78), the 'Gorgeous Gael', was a British army guardsman, boxer, wrestler, singer and playboy. His marriage to Mexican film star Movita brought him world headlines when the two became a singing duet. After heady years of high living, he died destitute in London.

P.V. Doyle (1923–88) was a hotelier of note. Having established a chain of popularly priced establishments in the Dublin area, he built two in the luxury class.

Novelist, playwright and scriptwriter Roddy Doyle won the Booker Prize for his novel *Paddy Clarke Ha Ha Ha* (1993) and some of his books were adapted to become popular films.

DUFFY
Docy, Doocy, Doohey, Doohig, Dowey, *Duff*, Duhig, O'Diff, Ó Doithe, Ó Dubhthaigh, O'Duffy, O'Duhig

Motto: Deo juvante (God helping)

From *dubh*, meaning 'black', Duff is an abbreviation but is also a surname in its own right. Counties Roscommon and Donegal had O'Duffy septs but the name was most common in Monaghan. Nowadays, Dowey and Doohey are most often found in Donegal, while the variant Duhig is mainly of Munster origin.

At the start of the sixteenth century, Tadhg O'Duffy recorded two O'Duffys, Cadhla and Muireadach, as being early archbishops of Tuam. Fr Eugene O'Duffy (1527–1615) was a noted preacher and satirist.

Young Irelander Sir Charles Gavan Duffy (1816–1903) was co-founder and editor of *The Nation* and was a land reform agitator and MP for New Ross, County Wexford. His son George (1882–1951) befriended Roger Casement and prepared his defence in 1916. Later, George was TD for South Dublin (1918–23) and was the last plenipotentiary to sign the Treaty. He became Minister for Foreign Affairs in the Provisional Government of 1922 and later was President of the High Court. His sister Louise (1884–1969) taught in Padraic Pearse's Scoil Íde and founded the Irish-language Scoil Bhríde.

Duffy's Circus has been touring Ireland since 1776.

More recently

Frank Duff (1889–1980) founded the Legion of Mary in 1921. He was active in closing Dublin's red-light district known as 'Monto'.

During the Irish War of Independence, General Eoin O'Duffy (1892–1944) was IRA Director of Organisation and later Chief of Staff, succeeding General Richard Mulcahy. He was Commissioner of the Civic Guard (later Garda Síochána) and in the 1930s became leader of the Blueshirt movement. He organised the Irish Brigade that supported General Franco in the Spanish Civil War.

County Monaghan man Bernard Duffy (1882–1952) wrote comic plays for the Abbey Theatre.

Musician Keith Duffy of the band Boyzone was a popular inmate of the 2001 *Celebrity Big Brother* TV series.

DUNNE
Dineen, Dun, Dunn, Kildunn, Ó Doinn, O'Doyne, Ó Duinn, O'Dunne

Motto: Mullach Abú (Forever highest/The summit forever)

The motto is that of the O'Dunn. *Donn* simply means 'brown'. A County Laois sept, the chieftain was Lord of Iregan. Dunnes had a reputation for ferocity in battle. The O'Dunn or Dunn form is found mainly in Ulster. Dunne is an English name also.

Giolla-na-Naomh (saints' messenger or servant) Ó Dúnn (or Ó Duinn, 1102–60) was the Chief Poet of Leinster, whose work appears in the Book of Ballymote. He wrote extensively about Milesians, kings and their resting-places.

A medieval scholar who emerged from obscurity to feature on an Irish pre-euro banknote may have had Dunn roots. Both Ireland and Scotland have claimed Johannes Duns Scotus (1266–1308). A prolific commentator on theology, logic and metaphysics, he wrote in Latin. Yet his supporters faced accusations of backwardness in learning, so begetting the word 'dunce'.

In the US, Judge Charles Dunn (1799–1872) was an esteemed figure. Colonel Humphrey O'Dunne displayed gallantry against the forces of Brigadier General Clinton at Savannah during the War of Independence (1775–83).

Sir Patrick Dun (1642–1713) was born on Inn's Quay, Dublin, and lived later in Skinner Row. He moved to Scotland (some sources say he was born there) and became an army chaplain in the late seventeenth century. MP and five times President of the Royal College of Physicians in Ireland, he left a bequest that established a hospital that bore his name on Grand Canal Street, Dublin.

More recently

New York cornet player Johnny Dunn (1897–1937) was a popular recording star until he had the temerity to challenge Louis Armstrong in public. 'Satchmo' could be a formidable antagonist and he used his influence to deny Dunn engagements, thus shattering his career.

Eileen Dunne is a popular long-term newsreader on RTÉ television. Her father, Michael, was a Gaelic games commentator, also with RTÉ.

Veronica Dunne, singer, has taught and encouraged young talent and started them on classical singing careers.

And the Irish, passing a compliment on any successful outcome, remark '"Well done," said Old Dunne when Young Dunne was born.'

FITZGERALD
FitzGerald, Mac Gearailt

Motto: Crom Abú (Crom forever)

Crom Dubh was a harvest deity and Crom Dubh Castle near Hospital, County Limerick, was a Fitzgerald stronghold. Fitzgeralds are omitted from families followed by the banshee because they had a distinguished personal harbinger of death – the sun goddess Áine, no less!

Gearaltach means Geraldine. Some sources claim a common ancestor: Gerald, Constable of Pembroke and husband of Nesta, Princess of Wales. His son, Maurice, joined with Strongbow in the Anglo-Norman invasion. Fitz is from the French *fils* (son).

The powerful settlers held, in Desmond, the knightships of Kerry and of Glin. The County Kildare leaders held sway up to the execution of Silken Thomas (Lord Thomas Fitzgerald, Lord

Offaly and Tenth Earl of Kildare, 1513–37). Tradition tells that Katherine Fitzgerald, the Countess of Desmond, died in 1604 after falling from a fruit tree she was climbing at the age of 120.

Lord Edward Fitzgerald (1763–98) led a military committee of the United Irishmen who planned a rebellion assisted by a French invasion. He died of wounds received when resisting arrest in Thomas Street, Dublin.

Desmond FitzGerald (1888–1947) fought in the 1916 Rebellion and was imprisoned. He became a Sinn Féin MP in 1918 and was Director of Publicity for the First Dáil. During the Irish War of Independence he edited the underground *Bulletin*. He held the ministries of External Affairs (1922–27) and Defence (1927–32) and was a senator and author.

More recently

Actor William Joseph Shields (1888–1961) was better known by his stage name, Barry Fitzgerald. American critics raved about his performances with the Abbey Theatre on tour there. He won an Oscar and the hearts of millions for his playing of Fr Fitzgibbon in *Going My Way*. In *The Quiet Man*, he had another major success.

Dr Garret FitzGerald, son of Desmond (above), was Minister for Foreign Affairs (1973–77) and Taoiseach (1981–82 and 1982–87). An economist and writer, he later became director of a number of prestigious companies.

FITZPATRICK

Fitch, Fitchpatrick, FitzPatrick, Fitz-Patrick, Gilpatrick, Kilpatrick, Kirkpatrick, MacGilpatrick, Mac Giolla Phádraig, MacIlpatrick, MacKilpatrick, Paragon, Parogan, Parrican, Patchy, Patrician, Patrick

Motto: Ceart láidir Abú (Right and might forever)

Literally, Mac Giolla Phádraig means 'son of Patrick's servant or messenger' but it suggests a zealous follower of St Patrick. The surname has the distinction of being the only one using the prefix 'Fitz' with proven Gaelic-Irish origin. It was originally the Ossory sept of a belligerent tenth-century chieftain, Giolla Pádraig. Some of the many variations and corruptions are of Scottish origin and are found mainly in Ulster. Before the rise of the Ormond Butlers, Fitzpatricks were lords of Upper Ossory. They submitted to Henry VIII, and Sir Barnaby Fitzpatrick was knighted in 1568, during the reign of Elizabeth I.

Cromwell's army slaughtered Brian Fitzpatrick (1585–1652), Ossory's Vicar Apostolic who transcribed the 'Book of the O'Byrnes' (see Byrne), thus preserving it for posterity.

William John Fitzpatrick (1830–95) wrote biographies of a number of prominent personages like Lady Sydney Morgan, Bishop James Warren Doyle and Thomas Higgins ('The Sham Squire' who informed on Lord Edward Fitzgerald). He published an allegation that Thomas Scott and not his brother Sir Walter wrote the Waverley novels.

More recently

Bernard John ('BJ') Fitzpatrick chaired his large wholesale jewellery firm, B.J. Fitzpatrick & Co. Ltd (1937), and Irish Silver Ltd (1965). Also, he was a director of Waterford Glass, honorary trustee of the Company of Goldsmiths of Dublin, and warden and master of the Goldsmiths' Corporation of Dublin.

Down-born journalist and author W.J. Fitzpatrick (1902–82) recorded folk songs, tales and superstitions of the Mourne Mountains.

FLANAGAN
Flang, Flanigan, Flannagan, O'Flanagan, Ó Flannagáin

Motto: Certavi et vici (I have fought and conquered)

(For *flann*, see Flynn.) A Connaught Ó Flannagáin sept's chief was the hereditary 'Royal Lord' or steward to the province's kings, the O'Connors. There were less influential septs in Counties Offaly and Fermanagh.

The thirteenth/fourteenth-century Bishop of Elphin, Donough O'Flanagan (d. 1308), made himself a name internationally for being extremely pious and hospitable.

Fr Michael O'Flanagan (1876–1942) was a writer and activist on behalf of turf-cutters and on behalf of Sinn Féin, of which he became Vice-Chairman. He spoke at the O'Donovan Rossa lying in state (see Donovan) and prayed at the opening of the First Dáil (1919). An advocate of the struggle for independence, he was silenced on a number of occasions and participated in private peace negotiations with the British Prime Minister, David Lloyd George, in December 1920. He espoused Irish and Spanish republican causes in the US. From 1924 to 1942, he edited and prepared fifty volumes of Dr John O'Donovan's *Archaeological Survey of Ireland* and his *County Histories*.

Fr Edward J. Flanagan (1886–1948) from County Roscommon believed there was no such thing as a really bad boy. He founded 'Boys' Town', to care for neglected boys, in Omaha, Nebraska, in 1921. Playing the priest in the film *Boys' Town* won Spencer Tracy an Oscar in 1938.

More recently

Kevin O'Flanagan was a member of the Irish rugby team that achieved a grand slam, winning all international matches, in 1948. He was also a soccer international.

Oliver J. Flanagan (1920–87) was a colourful right-wing Laois–Offaly TD. His electioneering ploy was cycling with a sandwich-board on his back. The slogan 'Here comes Oliver' was on the front and 'There goes Oliver' was on the back. He was

Parliamentary Secretary for Fisheries (1954–57) and for Local Government (1975–76) and Minister for Defence (1976–77).

Fr Henry Flanagan OP of Droichead Nua Dominican College is a celebrated sculptor, particularly in wood.

FLYNN
Fleens, Flinn, Lynn, MacFlynn, Ó Floinn, O'Flynn, O'Lynn

Motto: Esse quam videre (To be, rather than to seem)

Irish poets used the word *flann* for blood but as an adjective it meant 'blood red', 'bloody', 'ruddy' or 'sanguinary'. Muiscre Uí Fhloinn was Irish for Muskerylinn, part of Muskerry where there were two septs. The other was in Corca Laoidhe. Flynns were henchmen of the Connaught O'Connors, who afforded them the honour of riding the chieftain's horse. The Lynn form developed mainly in Ulster, through aspirating the F of Floinn to give an L sound. The plight of one of that sept, found mainly east of Lough Neagh, is remembered in a ballad:

> Brian O'Lynn had no breeches to wear
> He got an old sheepskin to make him a pair,
> With the fleshy side out and the woolly
>   side in,
> 'By gosh! They are pleasant and cool,' says
>   O'Lynn.

In 1816 Fr Jeremiah Flynn (1788–1831) was the first Franciscan to be assigned to the Australian mission as a result of a petition to Rome by Fr Richard Hayes.

Edmund Flynn (1847–1927) was Premier of Quebec, Canada (1896–97).

William James Flynn (1867–1928) became head of the Federal Bureau of Investigation in the US.

'Flynn of the Inland' was an Australian flying doctor service founded by a Presbyterian missionary, John Flynn (1880–1951).

Cork-born Fr James Christopher O'Flynn (1881–1962) travelled the county on his motorcycle teaching and collecting traditional music. In a room over a sweet factory in Cork city, he established 'The Loft', through which many famous actors passed. During the month of May 1927, he directed six Shakespearean plays at Cork Opera House.

More recently

Irish-American Elizabeth Gurley Flynn (1890–1964) was Chairperson of the American Communist Party.

Swashbuckling screen hero Errol Flynn (1909–59) had a number of teenage mistresses.

Pádraig Flynn, European Commissioner, and his daughter Beverly Cooper Flynn TD from Castlebar, County Mayo, were politicians who gained some notoriety in the first years of the twenty-first century.

GALLAGHER

Callagher, Galagher, Gallacher, Gallaher, Gallaugher, Galligor, Galliher, Gallihur, Gallogher, Gallougher, Goligher, Gollagher, Gollocher, Gollogher, Golloher, Goloher, O'Gallagher, Ó Gallchobhair

No motto

Americans pronounce it Gallager, Galliger or Golligar. The root may be *gall chabhair* (meaning 'foreign help'). Around Ballybofey–Stranorlar and in the Raphoe area of County Donegal, the Ó Gallchobhairs held small territories that they populated densely. They spread to Sligo, Derry and Tyrone.

Descended from Niall of the Nine Hostages, many of their chieftains were officers in the forces of the O'Donnells. A number of Ó Gallchobhairs became bishops. One, in Derry diocese, was Bishop Redmond Ó Gallchobhair (1521–1601). He assisted survivors of the Spanish Armada wrecked off the north-east coast in 1588. Despite disguising himself as a shepherd and enjoying the protection of his spiritual flock, he could not avoid capture and execution.

Dr Thomas Gallagher (1851–1925) was a Fenian Dynamiter and its Director of Training in the US. Thomas Clarke was among his trainees. In 1883 the pair were captured while engaged in underground activities in England. Gallagher received a life sentence but just three years of extremely harsh conditions allegedly led to his derangement and release. He died in a sanatorium for the mentally ill.

Cottage Island on Lough Gill is also known as Gallagher's Island. A cottage there belonged to a mysterious woman named Beezie Gallagher (b. *c.* 1860), to whom were attributed many powers, including that of fostering romance between couples.

More recently

Bridie Gallagher was one of Ireland's most celebrated ballad singers.

Patrick 'Paddy the Cope' (co-op) Gallagher (1873–1964) was a pioneer of the co-operative movement and cottage industries in County Donegal.

In business, Gallaher (Dublin) Ltd became a major manufacturer and distributor of tobacco products.

Frank Gallagher (1898–1962) assisted Erskine Childers with the republican *Irish Bulletin* during the Irish War of Independence. He took the anti-Treaty side in the Irish Civil War. He was first editor of the *Irish Press*, Deputy Director of Radio Éireann and Director of the Government Information Bureau. He wrote two books on his experiences: *Days of Fear* (1928) under his own name and *The Four Glorious Years* (1953) using the pseudonym David Hogan.

HEALY

**Healey, Healihy, Heally, Heily, Hely, Hilo,
Kerisk, Kerrish, Kerrisk, Mac Fhiarais,
O'Haly, Ó hÉalaighthe, O'Healihy,
O'Healy, Ó hÉilidhe**

Motto: Strenue constanter et recte (Earnestly,
constantly and rightly)

The Irish form found in Munster (Ó hÉalaighthe)
suggests ingenuity, stealth or escape. That from
Connaught (Ó hÉilidhe) means a claim (*éileamh*).
Their seats, respectively, were at Donaghmore, near
Coachford, County Cork, and at Ballyhely, County
Sligo. There are three Ballyhealys and a Healysland
in Wexford too. Healy can also be a synonym of
Kerrisk or Kerrish (Mac Fhiarais). The name
appeared among the French nobility, in the family
of Hely d'Oissel.

John Hely (1724–94) added his heiress wife's
name (later Baroness Donoughmore) to become
Hely-Hutchinson, MP for Cork, Principal
Secretary of State and Provost of Trinity College
Dublin. His anonymous publication *Commercial
Restraints of Ireland* (1779) was condemned on
grounds of sedition. The common hangman was
ordered to burn it in public.

James Healy (1830–1900) was known as
America's first black bishop (Portland, Maine,
1875–1900). His father was an Irish immigrant,
his mother a mulatto slave.

More recently

Timothy Michael (Tim) Healy (1855–1931), Irish nationalist MP, was the first Governor General of the Irish Free State.

From Drogheda, County Louth, John E. Healy (1872–1934) spent twenty-seven years (1907–34) editing and writing leaders for *The Irish Times*. The same newspaper featured Mayo man John Healy (1930–91), author and journalist, whose 'Backbencher' column was highly regarded for its sharp political comment.

Stained-glass work by Michael Healy (1873–1941) appears in a number of locations throughout Ireland. He worked in Sarah Purser's celebrated An Túr Gloine (The Tower of Glass) studio.

HUGHES
Hews, Hughs, Mac Aodha, McCoy, MacHugh, MacKay, McKee, Ó hAodha, O'Hugh

Motto: Verus amor patriae (The true love of country)

Aodh was a personal name often spelt Áed but invariably Anglicised to Hugh. Cognate with the Latin *aedes* or *aestus*, it meant 'inflammation' or 'fire'.

Although of English and Welsh origin, the Anglicisation from Ó hAodha or Mac Aodha comes from Irish septs prominent in Ulster and in Counties

Meath and Galway. These were 'sons of Aodh',
whether kings, chieftains or saints from early history.

Hughes mottoes are mostly in Welsh. The
Latin version cited above is of a County Wexford
family. Those Anglicised to O'Hea came from
Corca Laoidhe and were genuinely Irish.
Thirteenth- and sixteenth-century bishops of Cork
and of Ross bore the name.

Tyrone-born John Hughes (1797–1864) was
first Archbishop of New York. A former gardener,
he supported the Union in the American Civil War
and travelled to Europe to promote its cause. He
founded the college that became Fordham
University, New York.

William Morris Hughes (1862–1952) was
British-born Prime Minister of Australia from 1915
to 1923.

John Hughes (1865–1941) sculpted the statue
of Queen Victoria that once stood outside Leinster
House. Charles Kickham (in Tipperary) and
William E. Gladstone (Hawarden, Clwyd, Wales)
were other subjects. He exhibited at International
Exhibitions in Dublin, Paris and Brussels.

More recently

Billionaire Howard Hughes (1905–76) lent
$200,000 to Richard Nixon's brother Donald. 'The
Hughes Loan' dogged Nixon's early political career.

Micheál Ó hAodha (1918–98) was one of the
last pupils of a hedge-master in County Clare. He
was an author, playwright, broadcaster, radio

producer and Abbey Theatre director. He wrote the theatre's first Irish pantomime, *Muireann agus an Prionnsa*, and biographies of Micheál mac Liammóir and of Siobhán McKenna.

KANE
Cahan, Cain, Cane, *Kean, Keane*, McCahan, McCahane, MacCloskey, MacEvinney, McKane, O'Cahan, Ó Catháin, Ó Céin, O'Kane

Motto: Felis demulcta mitis (A stroked cat is gentle)

Cath means 'battle' and Cathán (warrior) was a Dalcassian personal name. In Ulster, it became a surname for a sept whose influence lasted up to the province's plantation. County Antrim had an early St Cathán too. Keane (Ó Céin) is often substituted for Kane but can also be a variant of O'Cahan, which was the first Anglicisation of Ó Catháin. Others followed, and a rough guide in a complex situation has Keanes and its derivatives in Munster, with Kanes and theirs elsewhere except in Ulster. There, O'Kanes were most common.

Fishing communities once believed that a Donegal Kane begot seals and that the creatures would all become men one day. The celebrated cow of folklore, Glas Ghaibhne (Grey Cow of Gabhne), was in the care of three Kane brothers. The youngest lost the cow. Searching for it, he learned that Balor of the Evil Eye, a giant with an eye in the centre of his forehead, had the beast. Recovery would entail young Kane's sleeping with 300 red-haired women, 300 blondes and 300 brunettes. After nine months, each would give birth and one child would be Balor's grandson and eventual assassin. This came to pass and the child that killed his grandfather was Lugh of the Long Arm. The rest of the Kanes were tossed into the sea to become seals.

Domhnal Ballagh O'Cahan, the last sept chieftain, died a prisoner in the Tower of London in 1617.

Echlin O'Kane (1720–90) was a celebrated bard and harper.

Sir Robert John Kane (1809–90) was a scientist who studied university education methods and became President of Queen's College, Cork, and later Vice-Chancellor of the Royal University of Ireland. He participated in an inquiry into the potato blight and distresses resulting from the Great Famine that it caused.

More recently

Marie Keane was an Abbey Theatre actress who also starred in films and on radio.

John B. Keane is a popular playwright and author.

Terry Keane was a society columnist who admitted to being mistress of Charles J. Haughey, Taoiseach.

KAVANAGH

Caomhánach, Cavan, Cavanagh, Cavenagh, Kavenagh, Keevan, Keevane, Kevane, Keveney, Kivnahan

Motto: Siothcháin agus fairsinge (Peace and plenty)

Dónal, son of Dermot MacMurrough, lived at the monastery of St Caomhán (*caomh* means 'dear' or 'gentle') in County Wexford and so emerged the name Kavanagh. As an epithet, it never received the 'Mac' or 'O' indicating offspring. Found all over Ireland, the name is most common in Counties Wexford and Carlow.

Art MacMurrough Kavanagh, who died around 1417, was virtual King of Leinster. An overlord who, although raising black rent, received praise-poetry, he resisted stoutly the army of Richard II.

Without arms or legs, Arthur MacMurrough Kavanagh (1831–89) wrote and painted and was expert in yachting, fishing, horse riding and jumping with the aid of a chair-saddle. He travelled widely and participated in tiger hunts. He became MP for Carlow and for Wexford.

One of the Wild Geese, Art Kavanagh became Governor of Prague (1776) and was reputed to be the biggest man in Europe.

More recently

Raconteur 'Kruger' (Muiris) Kavanagh (1894–1971) was publicity manager for MGM and

impresario for acts like tenor Walter Scanlan.
He supervised auditions for the *Ziegfeld Follies*
and was bodyguard for Eamon de Valera's tour of
the US (1919–20).

Later, autographed pictures of great stars
decorated his Dún Chaoin inn. Brendan Behan
wrote a song in his praise. Once, however, he
became bored by Kavanagh's boasting about the
signed photographs 'To Kruger with love, from
Greta Garbo' and the like. As Behan was leaving
the inn, he took a pen and scrawled on a picture of
the Sacred Heart: 'To Kruger, from Jaysus'.

The poet Patrick Kavanagh (1904–67)
probably is most famous for the long poem
outlining the harshness of rural life, *The Great
Hunger* (1942), or for the song:

> On Raglan Road on an autumn day I met her
>   first and knew
> That her dark hair would weave a snare that I
>   might one day rue.

KELLY
**Kealy, *Keely*, Keily, *Kilkelly*, MacKelly,
Ó Caollaidhe, Ó Ceallaidhe, Ó Ceallaigh,
O'Kelly, Queally**

Motto: Turris fortis mihi Deus (God is a strong
tower to me)

Probably derived from *ceallach*, meaning 'recluse',
'hermit', 'churchgoer', 'bright-headed' or 'conflict',

Kelly is the second most numerous name in
Ireland. A chieftain bearing the personal name
Ceallach has claim on the origin too. The name
spread from areas like Uí Máine, whose Kellys
alone are entitled to the motto above. County
Sligo, the Four Tribes of Tara and the Seven Septs
of Laois included O'Kellys too. From The O'Kelly
of Cenél Eachrach sprang those of Ulster, mainly
in Antrim and Derry. Dublin's many Ó Ceallaighs
originated in Wicklow. In the south-east of the
country the common form intermingled with
Ó Ceallaidhe, Keily, Kealy and Queally (Tipperary,
Kilkenny, Waterford and Wexford, respectively).

The O'Kelly of Uí Máine, however, was the
progenitor. Fourteenth-century chieftains of the
sept were renowned for hospitality and from their
lavish entertainments evolved the term 'O'Kelly's
Welcome'. Later, they became a feared family and
the Corporation of Galway proclaimed them as
such in 1518. Enemies avoided 'O'Kelly Country'
in Galway and Roscommon. Since 1601 The
O'Kelly of Gallagh has been recognised as Chief of
the Name. A castle on a hill there was burned in
1504. A Blakeney family rebuilt it and it became
known as Castleblakeney but retained the
connection in the Irish form Gallach Uí
Cheallaigh. Sir Percival 'Percy' Blakeney inspired
'The Scarlet Pimpernel'.

The small diocese of Clonfert in east Galway
had no fewer than four bishops of the name.

Edward (Ned) Kelly (1855–80) was a notorious bushranger and bank robber in the south-eastern region of Australia who was eventually captured and hanged.

Mary Eva Kelly or 'Eva of *The Nation*' (1826–1910) contributed nationalist verse to a number of publications.

Kelly or Kelley is often used as a girl's name, particularly in the United States. There, too, Michael Kelly (1857–94) was a baseball hero and 'Honest John' Kelly ruled the Democratic Party's Tammany Hall from 1871 to 1886. Although accused of underhanded dealings, he introduced some reforms to its tarnished image.

In 1878 an Irish woman, Madame Kelly, founded her 'House of all Nations', the *Chabanis* in Paris that became the city's most famous brothel.

Representing England, Cork man George Con O'Kelly won the Olympic wrestling heavyweight title in 1908.

More recently

Playwright An tAthair Tomás Ó Ceallaigh (1879–1924), Professor of Education at University College Galway, translated the W.B. Yeats play *Cathleen ni Houlihan* into the Irish *Caitlín Ní h-Uallacháin*.

Seán T. Ó Ceallaigh (1882–1966) was President of Ireland from 1945 to 1959. Pope Pius XI awarded him the Grand Cross of St Gregory the Great.

Eamon Kelly (1914–2001), husband of actress Maura O'Sullivan, appeared in numerous plays and films but was best known for his one-man performances as a *seanchaí*.

Oisín Kelly (1915–81) sculpted the statues of Jim Larkin in Dublin's O'Connell Street and the Children of Lir grouping in the city's Garden of Remembrance.

John B. Kelly (d. 1960), father of film star Grace (1929–82), won over 100 rowing events, including three Olympic gold medals.

In June 1965, folk singer Luke Kelly (1940–84) married Focus Theatre director and actress Deirdre O'Connell (1939–2001) in the Merrion Inn, Dublin. Kelly's performance of Phil Coulter's 'The Town I Loved so Well' and 'Scorn Not his Simplicity' and of Patrick Kavanagh's 'Raglan Road' is definitive.

And, finally, the personification of the Irish in New York probably will always be the fictitious girl that the city's police were all so mad about – 'Little Nellie Kelly'.

KENNEDY
Keenedy, Kenady, Minnagh, Ó Cinnéide, O'Kennedy, Quenedy

Motto: Avis(e) la fin (Look to the end)

Ceann (head), *éidigh* (ugly): not a flattering translation but there can be no other for the

Dalcassian sept that originated along the County Clare coastline and north of the Shannon estuary. Killokennedy in County Clare perpetuates the memory of the sept's foundation. Brian Boru's father and nephew bore the name. O'Brien and MacNamara harassment drove them across to Tipperary. Then to Kilkenny, where as lords of Ormond they resisted the usurping Butlers for 500 years. During that time (eleventh to sixteenth centuries) An Cinnéide Don, Rua and Fionn emerged. They spread to Wexford and south Wicklow. Some reached Dublin and Antrim.

Synonyms originated in Leitrim and in Spain, where Kennedys fought.

Newtownmountkennedy in Wicklow boasted the longest name of a town in Ireland until a small townland in north Kildare (Newtownmoneenaluggagh) challenged it. The former is called after a nearby motte, Mount Kennedy, which stands on lands granted to Sir Robert Kennedy in 1671.

Donegal man John Pitt Kennedy (1796–1879) was an army engineer who retired and pioneered agricultural education in Ireland. Disillusioned, he re-enlisted at the invitation of Sir Charles Napier, Commander-in-Chief in India, and built a great military road from the Simla Plains towards Tibet.

Under his pseudonym Harry Whitney, Patrick Kennedy (1801–73) from County Wexford kept a bookshop in Anglesea Street, Dublin. He sold his own sketches and miscellanies of Irish rural life but was also published by Macmillan and by M'Glashan and Gill. *Legends of Mount Leinster*, *Fireside Stories of Ireland* and *Legendary Fictions of the Irish Celts* were among his most popular works.

More recently

Hugh Kennedy (1879–1936) was Honorary Secretary of the Árd Craobh of the Gaelic League. He helped draft the Constitution of the Irish Free State, of which he was the first Attorney General and first Chief Justice. Also, he became a governor of the National Gallery of Ireland.

US President John Fitzgerald Kennedy (1917–63), son of wealthy industrialist and diplomat Joe, was assassinated in Dallas, Texas. His brother, Robert Francis (1925–68), US Attorney General, was also assassinated, in Los Angeles, California, while campaigning for the Democratic nomination as a presidential candidate. Their great-grandfather was from Dunganstown, County Wexford. President Kennedy visited there in June 1963. Before his departure from Shannon Airport, reading from a note given to him by President Eamon de Valera's wife, Sinéad, he misquoted Gerald Griffin's poem that accurately goes:

> 'Tis, it is the Shannon's stream
> Brightly glancing, brightly glancing!
> See, oh see the ruddy beam
> Upon its waters dancing

To see old Shannon's face again,
Oh, the bliss entrancing.

The departing statesman added 'Well, I am going to see old Shannon's face again.' He never did.

Jimmy Kennedy (1902–84) of Tyrone, later of Portstewart, County Derry, wrote popular songs like 'The Teddy Bears' Picnic', 'Red Sails in the Sunset' and 'South of the Border'. His 'Cokey-Cokey' later became a dance called the 'Hokey-Cokey'.

LYNCH
Leyne, Linchy, Lynchy, Mac (or O') Lynchehan, Ó Loingsigh

Motto: Semper constans et fideli (Ever constant and faithful)

Ar an luing seo, Páid Uí Loingsigh
Bhímse ag déanabh bróin
Ag osnáil gach aon oíche
Is go síoraí ag sileadh deóir.

On the deck of Paddy Lynch's boat
I was in woeful sorrow
Sighing every single night
And crying each tomorrow.

The anonymous early Irish poem combines the root and the name, because *loingseach* means 'seaman' or 'mariner', 'pirate' or 'sea rover'. That settles the Irish question but Norman de Lenchs were greater in number and in influence. Paramount among the Tribes of Galway, the name is perpetuated in that city by Lynch's Castle.

In 1493, tradition tells, Mayor James Lynch condemned his own son to hanging for murdering a Spanish youth. The term 'Lynch Law' may have stemmed from this incident, but there are other claims (see below). Between 1485 and 1654, Galway city had eighty-four mayors named Lynch. Many city wardens, appointed by a papal bull, were Lynchs too.

In education, Mayor Dominick Lynch founded, in 1580, a school at the city's harbour. It became a centre of nationalist activities and of Roman Catholic culture. Suppressed by James I in 1615, it flourished again under that king's son, Charles I, when another Lynch, Alexander, supervised up to 1,250 pupils. The figure still grew and the corporation was forced to order lashing of all 'foreigne beggars and poor schollers' until the city was rid of them. Fr John Lynch (1599–1673), author of *Cambrensis Eversus*, taught there.

The many feats of explorer Henry Blosse Lynch (1807–73) included the first navigation of the river Tigris as far as Baghdad in Iraq. After the Persian War, he helped negotiate the Treaty of Paris in 1857, so earning membership of the Order of the Lion and Sun from the Shah of Persia. His younger brother Thomas Kerr (1818–91) explored the same area and established steamer travel on the Tigris.

There were Lynchs in all four provinces, with strong septs holding lands in Thomond and Dalriada. A member of the Breffny sept, Dr J.J. Lynch (1816–88), was Bishop of Toronto. Some claim his strict regime coined the phrase 'Lynch Law' and the word 'lynching'. But there is another American version of this. It tells that in the seventeenth century, Piedmont, West Virginia, was an isolated district and that a citizen, James Lynch, received authority to conduct trials there.

The 'Foremost Chilean naval hero' was Patricio Lynch and Elizabeth Lynch ruled Paraguay.

Dr John Lynch was an American Civil War chaplain, while Thomas Lynch signed the nation's Declaration of Independence.

Château-Bages Lynch is a respected Bordeaux wine with an Irish Lynch background.

Liam Lynch led the anti-Treaty forces during the Irish Civil War. He was wounded in action on the Knockmealdown Mountains, County Tipperary, in 1923 and died later in Clonmel Hospital, thus precipitating the ending of the war.

More recently

Patricia Lynch (1898–1972) was a popular author of children's books, particularly *The Turf Cutter's Donkey* (1934).

Charles Lynch (1906–89) was a celebrated concert pianist from Cork who assisted conductor Sir Thomas Beecham with the Hallé, London and Royal Philharmonic orchestras.

Jack Lynch (1917–2000), accomplished Cork hurler and footballer with All-Ireland medals in both codes, was Taoiseach from 1966 to 1973 and from 1977 to 1979.

MacCARTHY
Carthy, *Carton*, Carty, Charthy, McArthy, Mac Cárthaigh, McCarthy, *O'Carthy*

Motto: Virtus invicta (Virtue unconquered)

From *carthanach*, meaning 'charitable', 'loving' or 'friendly', the leading Munster sept was chief among the Eoghanacht, particularly in Muskerry and West Carbery.

Of the many Irish names preceded by 'Mac' this is by far the most common. It is interesting to note that the name Justin – often given to MacCarthy boys – is an Anglicised form of Saorbreathach (noble judge). He was father of the chieftain of the Eoghanacht, Cárthach. Flurry, or Flor (Florence) and Fineen are other personal names that prominent MacCarthys have borne – often with pride but sometimes in disgrace – down the centuries.

The MacCarthy Mór occupied Killarney and other parts of County Kerry. The famous lakes were part of the sept's Muckross estate (now a National Park).

Cormac MacCarthy built the early twelfth-century 'Cormac's Chapel' within the outcrop of the Rock of Cashel.

Florence (Fineen) MacCarthy (Lord Carbery, 1572–1640) wrote a history of early Ireland while serving a sentence in the Tower of London for attempting to extend his Carbery territory through marriage. Yet, a number of MacCarthys paid homage to monarchs and received earldoms in return.

King Louis XVI ennobled Justin Count MacCarthy (1744–1812), a celebrated bibliophile in France.

Cork-born politician, author and journalist Justin MacCarthy (1830–1912) became MP for Longford in 1879 and later was vice-chairman of Parnell's Irish Party. Although remaining friendly with his leader, he led the anti-Parnell faction when Captain William O'Shea, seeking a divorce from his wife Katherine (Kitty), named Parnell as the co-respondent. His son, Justin Huntley (1860–1936), was also a nationalist MP, author and playwright whose subjects included Irish and Oriental myth and legend.

Under the battlements of Cormac Láidir (Strong Cormac) MacCarthy's fifteenth-century Blarney Castle is the stone that millions kiss, hoping for the 'gift of the gab' or Irish 'blarney'. F.S. Mahony (Father Prout: see Mahony) wrote:

A stone that whoever kisses

O, he never misses

To grow eloquent.

The McCarthy Cup has been the trophy for the All-Ireland Hurling Championship since 1921. It is named after Liam McCarthy, who fostered the game in Britain.

More recently

'McCarthyism' became a by-word for the investigations carried out by the US Republican Senator Joseph Raymond McCarthy (1909–57) on people suspected of subversion or of having communist sympathies. The Senate censured him in 1954.

Raconteur publican Mick McCarthy introduced pub theatre to Ireland in his Embankment pub in Tallaght, County Dublin.

MacLOUGHLIN

Laurence, *Loughlin*, McClachlin, MacGloughlin, McGloughlin, McLachlin, McLauchlin, MacLaughlin, McLaughlin, Mac Lochlainn, McLochlin, McLoghlen, McLoghlin, McLoughlan, McLoughlin, O'Loghlen, *O'Loughlin*

Motto: Cuimnigh ar do gheallamhnacha
(Remember your promises)

Lochlannach means 'Norseman' and was a personal name that became Anglicised to Loughlin or Laughlin, even to Laurence. Up to the third century Lochlannach was a leading branch of the Uí Néill in Tirchonaill, especially on the Inishowen peninsula. As a general rule, Ulster families used the MacLaughlin form. Elsewhere, MacLoughlin is more common. The latter superseded O'Mealaghlin (Ó Maoilsheachlainn), an Irish line descended from the celebrated King Malachy.

Once prominent in the midlands (especially County Meath), the Anglo-Norman invasion dissipated their power and at the start of the eighteenth century those remaining there predominantly used the Mac (or Mc) Loughlin form.

O'Loghlen was a County Clare form of spelling but it is important to point out that O'Loughlin was a separate Dalcassian sept.

In 1088, Dónal Mac Lochlainn, King of Oileach, destroyed Kincora, the seat of Dalcassian and Thomond kings.

John MacLoughlin (1784–1857), 'Father of Oregon', developed the old Indian methods of beaver trapping for the fur trade. He made Fort Vancouver near Portland an important port and he became a leading executive in its Hodson Bay Company that specialised in furs and hat-making. Fort Vancouver is now a National Historic Site.

North Californian Maurice McLoughlin, the 'Californian Comet', took tennis from the aristocracy, making it an offensive game with popular appeal. His 'American Twist' service won him the national title in 1913 and 1914 and gained him a place on US Davis Cup teams.

More recently

Engineer Thomas A. McLaughlin (1896–1971) conceived the Ardnacrusha, County Limerick, hydro-electricity power station on the lower Shannon. He left a lucrative appointment in Siemens-Schuckert, Germany, to become first Managing Director of the Electricity Supply Board. He led a team that prepared a report for the introduction of the Rural Electrification Scheme.

Joseph McLaughlin (1917–99), better known by his stage name Josef Locke, was a popular tenor, becoming famous for his spirited performance of songs like 'Blaze Away', 'The Soldier's Dream' and 'Jerusalem'. His performance of 'Violetta' inspired the film *Hear my Song*.

MAGUIRE
Macgivir, MacGuire, McGuire, Mag Uidhir, Mag Uidhre

Motto: Pro Deo et patria (For God and country)

Uidhre is the genitive of *odhar*, meaning 'dun' or 'greyish brown'. It also means a dun cow, so *Leabhar na hUidhre* is the Book of the Dun Cow. The Mag Uidhir seat was in Enniskillen and, despite plantations and confiscations, Fermanagh has always been a Maguire stronghold. The Mc form was found mainly in Connaught.

Hugh Maguire, Baron of Enniskillen, fought

valiantly at the Yellow Ford (1598), while Conor
(1616–45) was executed for treason. There were
Maguires among the Wild Geese and in religion; at
least three were bishops. Fr Thomas Maguire
(1792–1847) was the first Roman Catholic elected
to a Trinity College Dublin fellowship.

Conor Maguire (1889–1971) helped draft the
Constitution and Rules for Sinn Féin's Republican
Courts. He was a Republican Courts Judge, Land
Settlement Commissioner, Attorney General and
Chief Justice.

Sam Maguire from Dunmanway, County Cork,
who recruited Michael Collins into the IRB in
London, gave his name to the trophy for the All-
Ireland Gaelic Football Championship.

More recently

County Cavan-born musician Seán McGuire
broadcast at home and in Britain, the US and
Canada. Wurlitzers in New York invited him to
come and play their Stradivarius and Guarnarius.

Patrick Leo Maguire (1903–85) began
broadcasting in 1927. He wrote songs and dramas.
For thirty years his parting words for listeners to
the *Walton Programme* on Radio Éireann were:
'If you feel like singing, do sing an Irish song' –
one like the comic admonishment of a son by
his mother:

> Johnny get up from the fire, get up and give
> the man a seat.

Don't you know it's Mr Maguire and that he's
   courting your sister Kate.
Ah, you know very well he owns a farm a little
   bit out of town;
Well get up out of that you impudent brat and
   let Mr Maguire sit down.

Edward McGuire (1932–86) exhibited at home
and abroad. He painted portraits of Francis Stuart,
Patrick Kavanagh and Séamus Heaney.

And where would we be without a Maguire &
Patterson match?

MAHONY

Mahon, Mahoney, *McMahon*, O'Mahoney, O'Mahony, Ó Mathghamhana, Ó Mathúna

Motto: Per ardua surgam (I will rise through
difficulties)

Mathghamain (mod.: *mathúin*) means 'bear'. A sept
in west Munster bore the name that still
outnumbers the derivation and more modern
McMahon or Mahon. Mathghamhan of Thomond
was Brian Boru's grandson, and Counties Clare,
Monaghan and Leitrim contain all forms of the
name in considerable numbers. Cork, however, had
a number of O'Mahony strongholds.

Count Daniel O'Mahony fought with the Irish
Brigade of France at Cremona in the War of the
Spanish Succession (1701–14). He was the hero of

the battle, and was chosen to convey reports to King Louis XIV. He was promoted to the rank of colonel and all the officers and men of the Irish units received increases in pay.

The writer Francis S. Mahony (1804–66) was a hospital chaplain in Cork during a cholera epidemic. A disagreement with his bishop led to his leaving the priesthood. He used the pen-name 'Father Prout' and this causes confusion, because a genuine Fr Prout was Parish Priest of Watergrasshill, County Cork. Father Prout's most beloved verse was 'The Bells of Shandon'.

> With deep affection and recollection,
> I often think of those Shandon bells,
> Whose sound so wild would, in days of
>   childhood,
> Fling round my cradle their magic spells.

John O'Mahony (1816–77), Fenian and classical and Irish scholar, joined with William Smith O'Brien in an attempted rebellion in 1848. He founded the Fenian Brotherhood from which emerged the IRB.

More recently

Danno O'Mahoney became undisputed world champion wrestler in 1937. The 6 foot 2 inch ex-army man developed a throw that became known as the 'Irish Whip'.

Like the bards of old, Eoin 'The Pope' O'Mahony (1904–70) liked to visit and stay with friends whom he then regaled with wisdom, story and fable. A barrister by profession, he was a genealogist, lecturer and orator. His *Meet the Clans* was a popular radio programme.

MOORE
More, More O'Farrell, Morey, Ó Mordha, O'More

Motto: Conlán Abú (Oneself forever)

Mordha means 'great' or 'exalted' but it is Irish for O'More, a name that was distinct from Moore but has become almost extinct. Nowadays, More is used more as a personal name. Twenty-first in descent from a Red Branch Knights hero Conal Cearnach, Mordha is the eponymous ancestor. O'More was the foremost of the Seven Septs of Laois but Moore (moor – heather-covered open ground) was predominantly English or Anglo-Norman. The name appears mostly in Munster and in Counties Dublin and Antrim but has a generous scatter throughout Ireland.

The English saint, author and martyr Sir Thomas More (1478–1535) had proven connections with the Irish Moores of Barmeath, County Louth.

Two O'Moores named Rory were prominent in resistance to Tudor oppression. Another was installed at Ballina, County Kildare, in 1649. This Rory O'More enlisted the help of Owen Roe O'Neill in a bid to seize Dublin Castle during a general uprising. Treachery foiled the Dublin operation but Ulster rose. He commanded forces in the midlands until the arrival of Oliver Cromwell. Other Moores were officers in Continental armies, particularly in France.

Probably the most famous bearer of the name is Thomas Moore (1779–1852), the Dublin poet and composer of *Irish Melodies*.

George Henry Moore MP (1811–70) from Moore Hall in County Mayo supported Catholic tenants' rights and was an acclaimed orator. He founded the Catholic Defence Association. His novelist son, George A. (1852–1933), was associated with W.B. Yeats, Lady Augusta Gregory and Edward Martyn. Their combined activities in fostering an Irish revival led to the establishment of the Abbey Theatre. Another son and Connaught Ranger, Colonel Maurice Moore (1854–1939), fought in the Kaffir, Zulu and Boer wars. He campaigned for Home Rule and was Inspector General of the Irish Volunteers. A founder member of Fianna Fáil, he later became a senator.

More recently

Butch Moore (1938–2001) was Ireland's first entrant in the Eurovision Song Contest (1965) singing 'Walking the Streets in the Rain'.

From Newbridge, County Kildare, singer Christy Moore composes and sings protest songs as well as comic numbers.

And who can forget *Old Moore's Almanac*?

MORAN

**McMorran, Moarn, Moeran, Moren, Morin,
Morrin, Mourn, Murrin, Ó Mográin,
Ó Móráin, O'Moran, Ó Mugráin,
Ó Mugtáin, Ó Muireain, Ó Murcháin**

Motto: Lucent in tenebris (They shine in
darkness)

There is strong evidence that Moran, its derivatives
and synonyms originated from Ó Mugtáin and
Ó Mugráin septs in Galway and Roscommon
(Criffon and Ballintober) and from an Ó Móráin
sept around Ballina, County Mayo. The Galway and
Roscommon branches, however, may have belonged
to just one sept. Murrin and its synonyms came
from an Uí Fíachra family. The Offaly Ó Murcháins
spread to neighbouring counties. *Mór* (meaning
'big') seems to be the common root, but some
Morrins are of French and English origin.

General James O'Moran (1739–94) went to the
guillotine during the French Revolution.

Who from Faddle Alley off Dowker's Lane in
Dublin could gain fame but a balladeer? Michael
Moran (1794–1846) was better known as 'Zozimus'
because he recited the story of Blessed Zozimus
finding St Mary of Egypt after her fifty years of
penance in the desert. The saying 'St Patrick was a
Gentleman' came from one of his poem titles.

Patrick Francis Moran (1830–1911) of
Leighlinbridge, County Carlow, became

Archbishop of Sydney and increased its Roman Catholic flock by almost 100,000. He was Australia's first cardinal. Co-founder of the *Irish Ecclesiastical Record*, he also published a *Memoir of Oliver Plunkett* (1861).

Journalist David Patrick Moran (1871–1936) founded *The Leader* in 1900. Highly critical of existing language, literary and political establishments, he organised a 'Buy Irish' campaign.

More recently

Micheál Ó Móráin, Minister for Justice at the outset of the Arms Crisis, resigned (4 May 1970) on health grounds two days before An Taoiseach, Jack Lynch, dismissed Charles Haughey, Minister for Finance, and Neil Blaney, Minister for Agriculture.

The fictitious Dick Moran from RTÉ's soap opera *Glenroe* was probably Ireland's best-known philanderer.

MURPHY
Mac Murchadha, MacMurphy, Morphy, Murricohu, O'Morchoe, O'Muracha, Ó Murchú, O'Murphy, Ua Murchadha

Motto: Fortis et hospitalis (Brave and hospitable)

The most common name among the Irish at home or abroad is Murphy. Originally, the O and Mac prefixes appeared mainly in Ulster but all forms spread.

Murchad was an early Christian name (*muir* – sea, *cú* – hound: hound of the sea or sea warrior). Brian Boru had a son bearing it. The strongest Murphy sept was in Leinster, mainly in Counties Wexford, Wicklow and Carlow. They sprang from Dermot MacMurrough's brother, Murrough, progenitor of The O'Morchoe chieftains.

The name spread into Munster and became widespread in Kerry and Muskerry. That ancient territory bore Dahy (Dáithí) Ó Murchú, a blind sixteenth-century harper so famous that the celebrated pirate queen Granuaile (Grace O'Malley) travelled from Mayo to hear him play. Sligo, Tyrone and Donegal had their own distinct branches. Flaherty O'Murphy was a Donegal chieftain of note.

Domhnall Dall Ua Murchadha was Chief Sage of Leinster early in the twelfth century.

Seán Ó Murchadha (1700–62) was the last head of a celebrated Blarney Academy of Poets in Cork.

Cormacke Raver O'Murphy was an eighteenth-century Ulster highwayman who 'liked to run with the hares and hunt with the hounds'. In other words, he assisted the authorities in informing on others of his ilk while performing Robin Hood type of actions on behalf of the less fortunate.

Fr John Murphy (1753–98) was a hero of the 1798 Rebellion in Wexford. As the song 'Boolavogue' proclaims:

Then Father Murphy from old Kilcormac
Spurred up the rocks with a warning cry
'Arm, Arm,' he cried, 'for I've come to lead you.
For Ireland's freedom we'll fight or die.'

Irish Independent founder William Martin
Murphy (1844–1919) established the Dublin
Employers' Federation in 1911 and in 1913
dismissed Irish Transport and General Workers'
Union members whose champion was James
Larkin.

As time passed, the simple Anglicised form
Murphy took over almost completely. O and
Mac are seldom attached except in fiction (e.g.
Jack Nicholson's character in *One Flew Over the
Cuckoo's Nest*).

Hundreds of Murphys bear the nickname
'Spud', slang for a potato. A dubious yarn explains:
when Sir Walter Raleigh introduced the tuber
here, a certain Dr Murphy denounced the first
crop and organised opposition to it. His supporters
bore banners bearing the legend 'Society for the
Prevention of Unwholesome Diet' (SPUD).
Conversely, potatoes are sometimes called
'Murphys'.

More recently

With his machine-gun carrier 'Danny Boy',
Major General Humphrey Murphy, Officer
Commanding, Kerry No. 1 Brigade, was
prominent in suppressing anti-Treaty forces in
the south-west during the Irish Civil War.

A celebrated black stout from Cork is brewed by Murphys.

Seumas Murphy (1907–75) sculpted busts of Douglas Hyde, Michael Collins, Frank O'Connor, Seán Ó Riada and others.

Tom Murphy is a distinguished playwright and Dervla is a successful travel writer.

Delia Murphy (1902–71) was a popular singer of Irish ballads, particularly 'The Spinning Wheel' and 'Three Lovely Lassies'. In 1924 she married Irish diplomat Thomas J. Kiernan, who later served in London, the Vatican, Australia, West Germany, Canada and the US, so she endeared herself to the hearts of diplomats across the globe.

NOLAN
Holohan, Hulahun, Hultaghan, Knowlan, Knowland, Noland, Nolans, Nowlan, Ó hUallacháin, Ó hUltacháin, O'Nolan, Ó Nualláin

No motto

Nualláin is the genitive of *nuallán*, meaning a low cry or wail. *Nuall*, on the other hand, means a loud cry or clamour. Perhaps some were noisier than others! In any event, the origin is obscure.

O'Nolan, Prince of Foherta, led a sept holding office under early Leinster kings. Their power diminished after the Anglo-Norman invasion but branches that moved to Counties Mayo and Galway and to Corca Laoidhe gained some influence.

Philip Nolan (1771–1801) was an Irish-born mustanger and frontiersman. Son of Peter and Elizabeth (Cassidy) Nolan of Belfast, he was first in a line of filibusters who helped to free Texas from Spanish and Mexican rule. He produced an early map of the state. Living with Indians, dealing in mustangs, he corresponded with Thomas Jefferson about wild horse herds in Texas.

Colonel John Philip Nolan (1838–1912) served in Abyssinia. Elected MP for Galway in 1871, clerical intimidation unseated him. Re-elected in 1874, he introduced Parnell to the House of Commons.

More recently

Mrs Nolan attends Madame Flora's seance in Gian Carlo Menotti's opera *The Medium*. Mezzo-soprano Virginia Beeler created the role in 1946.

Ciarán Ó Nualláin (1910–83) wrote novels and essays in Irish. For twenty-five years he edited the Irish-language newspaper *Inniu*.

Seventh son of a seventh son, Finbarr Nolan became a celebrated faith healer, practising worldwide and administering to mass audiences as well as privately. In the 1970s he had an agent who had also worked for film stars Julie Andrews and Raquel Welch.

In 1988, quadriplegic author Christopher Nolan won the Whitbread Book Prize for *Under the Eye of the Clock*.

O'BRIEN

Brian, Brien, Briens, Brine, Brines, *Bryan*, *Crossan*, McBrien, Ó Briain, O'Brian, O'Bryan, O'Bryen, Uí Bhriain

Motto: Vigeur de dessus (Strength from above)

Proudly, O'Briens trace their origins to Brian Boru. Branches of the original Dalcassian clan, Uí Toirdealbhaigh, of which he was a member, took his name and spread all over Munster. Of these, many became powerful, notably those of Aherlow, of Thomond, of Pubblebrien (County Limerick), of Dromoland Castle and of Liscannor in County Clare. Sir Turlough O'Brien ruled the lands around Liscannor Bay. A few miles away, a monument still lauds Cornelius O'Brien, a nineteenth-century MP. This raconteur landlord from nearby Birchfield compelled his tenants to pay for the monument and build it themselves during his lifetime. To families whose comely girls gave him favours, folklore tells, 'Corny' showed his appreciation by increasing their holdings. A returned emigrant did not know this when he went walking one day and noticed one property that was much smaller than all the others. The *bean a' tighe* (woman of the house) was standing outside and he asked her why she had so few acres. The woman drew herself to full height and replied proudly, 'Because none of my daughters ever lifted their skirts above at the Big House.'

Such flippancy is, however, almost sacrilegious in chronicling a name that is scattered liberally across the pages of great historical works like the Annals of Innisfallen, Annals of Loch Cé, Annals of Ulster, Annals of Connaught, Annals of Tighernach and Annals of the Four Masters.

The regiment of France's Irish Brigade known as 'Clare's Dragoons' was raised by Daniel O'Brien, and the Fifth Viscount Charles O'Brien lost his life 'on Ramillies bloody field' in 1706. His successor, the Sixth Viscount, also Charles, fought at Dettingen (Germany) and at Fontenoy (Netherlands) and became a Marshal of France.

> When on Ramillies bloody field
> The baffled French were forced to yield
> The victor Saxon backward reeled
> Before the charge of Clare's Dragoons.
> The flags we conquered in that fray,
> Look lone in Ypres' choir, they say,
> We'll win them company today,
> Or bravely die like Clare's Dragoons.
> Viva La, the Old Brigade
> And Viva La, the new one too.
> Viva La, The Rose shall fade
> And the shamrock shine forever new.

County Clare nationalist William Smith O'Brien (1803–64) was a Conservative MP for County Clare but abandoned Daniel O'Connell to become a leading Young Irelander. O'Brien County in Iowa is named after him.

William O'Brien (1881–1968) of Clonakilty, County Cork, was a pioneering trade unionist and close associate of James Larkin and James Connolly. Secretary during the Lockout of 1913, he later participated in the 1916 Rebellion and endured imprisonment and hunger strike before becoming a TD.

More recently

Dermod O'Brien (1865–1945), painter, was President of the Royal Hibernian Academy and of the United Arts Club.

Flann O'Brien was a pseudonym for the brilliant humorist Brian Ó Nualláin (1911–66), who immortalised a favourite Irish beverage:

> When money's tight and is hard to get
> And your horse has also ran,
> When all you have is a heap of debt –
> A PINT OF PLAIN IS YOUR ONLY MAN

Kate (1897–1974), Richard Barry (1847–1918), Conor Cruise, Edna and other O'Briens became authors, scholars and political commentators, while broadcaster Tommy O'Brien (1905–88) of Clonmel made classical music popular.

Less lofty verse evoked by the name concerns a distracted father:

> Denis O'Brien had got three daughters fine
> The fairest young girls on the block.
> And between you and me, every night after tea
> To O'Briens the boys they would flock.

The upshot of this was that 'O'Brien had nowhere to go.'

O'CONNELL
Connell, Ó Congaill, Ó Connaill

Motto: Ciall agus neart (Reason and strength)

Literally, *connail* can mean either 'prudent' or 'kindly' but the origin is not clearly defined. Early septs became extinct. These were in Uí Máine, Oriel and in parts of Ulster and Connaught. Genealogists have traced the name back to Aengus Túirmeach, who was possibly a second-century High King. Later, a Magunihy chieftain bore the name.

Mention the name in Ireland and The Liberator, Daniel O'Connell (1775–1847), immediately springs to mind. His childless uncle, Maurice 'Hunting Cap' O'Connell, reared him. Daniel became champion of Catholic Emancipation and won renown for his resounding oratory at enormous rallies throughout the country. He was from Derrynane (or Darrynane), Caherdaniel, in County Kerry and from there too the main Gaelic sept originated. Their chieftain occupied the MacCarthy Mór castle at Ballycarbery, near Cahersiveen. The Cromwellian settlement displaced their seat to County Clare.

In 1767 Daniel O'Connell's aunt, Eibhlín Dhubh Ní Chonaill (*c.* 1743–1800), met and fell in love with Art O'Leary of Raleigh, Macroom, County Cork, a former officer in the army of Hungary. British forces killed him in 1773 and she wrote the acclaimed lament, 'Caoineadh Airt Uí Laoghaire'.

> *Mo gradh go daingean tú.*
> *Lá dá bhfaca thú*
> *Ag cheann tí an margaidh!*
> *Thug mo shúil aire dhuit,*
> *Thug mo chroí taithneamh duit,*
> *D'éalaíos óm' charaidh leat*
> *I bhfad ó bhaile leat.*

My unfaltering love to you.
The day I saw you
At the thatched market house!
My eye paid heed to you,
My heart took a liking to you,
I stole away from my friends with you
Far from my home with you.

J.J. 'Ginger' O'Connell (1887–1944) was Assistant Chief of Staff of the IRA at the time of the Truce. His kidnap by anti-Treaty forces was a significant factor in sparking off hostilities in the Irish Civil War.

More recently

One of a few large stones called Umbilicus Hiberniae or The Navel of Ireland (allegedly marking the country's centre) was at Seffin, County Offaly, until it was moved to Derrynane. It served as a Mass rock for the O'Connell household. The Laois–Offaly TD Oliver J. Flanagan had it returned to a site in Birr, County Offaly.

Mick O'Connell was a skilled Gaelic footballer for Kerry.

In 2001, Desmond Connell became the first Cardinal Archbishop of Dublin since Cardinal Paul Cullen in the nineteenth century.

O'CONNOR
Connor, Connors, Conor,
Mac Conchobhair, MacConnor,
Ó Conchuobhair, O'Conor

Motto: Ó Dhia gach aon cabhair (Every help from God)

While 'lover of wolves (or hounds)' and 'strong aid' have been suggested as translations of the personal name Conchobhair (Conor), there is little consensus on the origin of the surname. The motto belongs to the O'Connor Don only, an extant sept descended from the last High King of Ireland, Roderick O'Connor (1116–98). The other Connaught septs, O'Connor Sligo and O'Connor Roe, were also powerful.

The Munster O'Connors included the O'Connor Kerry who once controlled a vast area in the county. Their main fortification was at Carrigafoyle Castle near Ballylongford. They consolidated and held the area around it after

Anglo-Norman attacks. Nowadays, the name is still common in the Kerry–Cork region.

The Ballyvaughan–Corrofin–Liscannor area of County Clare was the land of the O'Connors of Corcomroe.

The O'Connor Faly led the County Offaly sept, traced back to Cathaoir Mór, Ireland's High King of the second century. Its war cry was 'Failiagh Abú'.

An early County Derry sept became extinct in the twelfth century. The name lives on in parts of the county, however.

Charles Owen O'Conor Don (1838–1906), the O'Conor Don, became Liberal MP for Roscommon, fostering the Roman Catholic cause there. An advocate of Home Rule and of Roman Catholic influence in education, he succeeded in introducing Irish as a subject on the Intermediate Board curriculum.

Charles O'Conor (1764–1828) was a librarian and antiquary. He produced a number of scholarly works, including the massive *Rerum Hibernicarum Scriptores Veteres* in four volumes.

Feargus Edward O'Connor (1794–1855), Repeal MP for Cork, split with Daniel O'Connell and lost his seat. In England, he became editor of the radical *Northern Star*, a Chartist leader and MP for Nottingham.

Rory O'Connor (1883–1922) was Director of Engineering with the IRA during the Irish War of Independence. He was a leader of the anti-Treaty forces in the Irish Civil War. He and three others were executed as a reprisal for the shooting of the pro-Treaty Major General Seán Hales TD.

The Connors form a leading branch of the travelling community in Ireland.

More recently

County Roscommon-born artist Roderic O'Conor (1860–1940) exhibited in Paris alongside Vincent van Gogh, Georges Seurat and Henri Raymond de Toulouse-Lautrec.

The Cork author and playwright Frank O'Connor (1903–66) was born Michael O'Donovan. His two-volume autobiography, biography of Michael Collins and translation of Brian Merriman's *Cúirt an Mheán Oíche* (*The Midnight Court*) received particular acclaim, as did his short stories. His witty translation, 'Advice to Lovers', says:

> The way to get on with a girl
> Is to drift like a man in a mist,
> Happy enough to be caught,
> Happy to be dismissed.
>
> Glad to be out of her way,
> Glad to rejoin her in bed,
> Equally grieved or gay
> To learn that she's living or dead.

Cardinal John O'Connor (1920–2000), the sometimes controversial Archbishop of New York, had Cork and Roscommon grandparents.

O'DONNELL

Daniel, Donnell, MacDonnell, _McDonnell,_
Ó Domhnaill

Motto: In hoc signo vinces (In this sign shall we
conquer)

'World powerful' is a possible translation for an
ancestor named Domhnall or Dónal, a descendant
of Niall of the Nine Hostages. Poems, plays and
pages of history remember the great Tirchonaill
sept. The name was powerful in Uí Máine,
Corcabaskin and in Thomond too.

The mid-sixth-century Domhnall Ilchelgach
('of the many treacheries') was an O'Neill and
MacLoughlin ancestor.

Sir Hugh O'Donnell's son, Red Hugh
(1571–1602), was a hero of Irish history. His
escape from Dublin Castle, his fight alongside
Hugh O'Neill at the Yellow Ford, his march to
Kinsale and his voyage to Spain are material of
legend. King Philip III of Spain honoured him in
life and posthumously, after poisoning at the hands
of a fellow countryman.

James Louis O'Donnell (1738–1811), Irish
Provincial of the Franciscan Order, later became
known as 'The Apostle of Newfoundland' where he
was Prefect and Vicar Apostolic.

'O'Donnell Abú' is a popular marching song
but in 1739, allegedly, a Roman Catholic priest
from County Donegal became a Protestant

minister, moving his mother to compose the lament:

> *Crádh ort, a Dhoimnic Uí Dhomhnaill*
> *Nach mairg ariamh a chonaic thú:*
> *Bhí tú 'do shagart Dia Domhnaigh*
> *'S ar maidin Dia Luain, 'do mhinister.*

Woe to you, Dominick O'Donnell
Ever woe to any who saw you:
You were a priest on Sunday
And on Monday morning, a minister.

Donegal man Cardinal Patrick O'Donnell (1856–1927) helped reunite nationalists after Parnell's death.

Peadar O'Donnell (1893–1986) was a revolutionary and distinguished writer. He organised the Irish Transport and General Workers' Union, fought in the Irish War of Independence, was imprisoned during the Irish Civil War and helped recruit for the anti-Franco International Brigade in the Spanish Civil War.

More recently

Liz O'Donnell TD, Minister of State at the Department of Foreign Affairs, was actively involved in the 1998 Good Friday Agreement negotiations.

Daniel O'Donnell is a popular singer and tea-party organiser!

O'FARRELL

Farrell, Farrelly, Ferrall, Ferrally, More O'Farrell, Ó Fearghail

Motto: Spes mea Deus (God is my hope)

The genealogy of its princes has been traced to Ir, the thirty-seventh line from Adam. Later ancestors were high kings of Ulster and of Ireland. The celebrated Queen Maeve was in the maternal lineage. A Longford descendant who fought with Brian Boru at Clontarf in 1014 earned the description that became the surname: Feargal (*fear* – man, *gal* – valour: man of valour). There were two distinct groupings – the O'Farrell Bán (white) and the O'Farrell Boy (*buidhe*: yellow).

Rulers of Annaly, the sept's seat was in Longford, so that the county town became Longphort Uí Fhearghail (Stronghold of the O'Farrells). In Ireland, the name spread mostly to the counties surrounding Longford but also countrywide, especially to Tyrone, Donegal, Wicklow, Offaly and Kildare. Abroad, it reached the Australian, European and American continents.

True to their name, many O'Farrells were soldiers, often distinguished officers who fell in battle or as a result of acts of treachery. Lieutenant General Richard O'Farrell, friend of Owen Roe O'Neill, fought in the rebellion of 1641 and in 1649 he defended Waterford against Cromwell for eight days. Cromwell withdrew but his son returned and O'Farrell negotiated honourable surrender terms.

In 1690, Ceadagh O'Farrell fell at the Battle of the Boyne.

Before the 1798 Battle of Ballinamuck, there was an attack on Granard. A verse remembers its hero:

In ninety-eight, from Ballinree
Brave Paddy Farrell rode
To bear his pike for Ireland free
Along the Granard road.

Abroad, three sons of Ceadagh O'Farrell (above) fought with the Irish Brigade in France. Richard O'Farrell fought and died at the Battle of the Little Big Horn. O'Farrells held commissions with the Irish Brigade in the Spanish Civil War and in the two world wars.

Some dispute More O'Farrells' being part of the sept. This may be because they were landlords. Richard More O'Farrell was MP for County Kildare from 1830 to 1847 and afterwards for County Longford. A descendant was murdered as late as 1935.

Fittingly, James P. Farrell founded *The Longford Leader* in 1897. He wrote *Historical Notes of County Longford* (1886) and *History of County Longford* (1891).

Nurse Elizabeth O'Farrell conveyed Padraic Pearse's surrender terms to the British Brigadier General Lowe at the end of the 1916 Rebellion in Dublin.

More recently

County Carlow-born author and broadcaster
Michael Farrell (1899–1962) was imprisoned
during the Irish War of Independence. He
contributed to *The Bell* and wrote *Thy Tears Might
Cease*, a manuscript that he found too unwieldy to
edit. Posthumously, Dr Monk Gibbon prepared it
for publication in 1963.

Playwright and novelist Molly Keane
(1904–96), née Mary Nesta Skrine, used the
pseudonym M.J. Farrell because she considered her
family and class would disapprove of her early light
comedies on the London stage. Later, she was a
member of Aosdána and at seventy-six years of age
she received a Booker Prize nomination for her
novel *Good Behaviour.*

O'LEARY
Lairy, Leary, Leery, Ó Laoghaire

Motto: Láidir is é Lear Righ (The King of the
Sea is strong)

'King of the sea' and 'Calf-herd' are likely
translations of Laoghaire. Originally a personal
name, it was also spelt Láegaire, Loegaire or Laoire.
Láegaire Mac Néill was an early King of Tara while
Láegaire Lorc and Láegaire Bern Buadach were
ancestors of Leinster and Ossory septs, respectively.
Dún Laoghaire is named after another Tara king
(sometimes Loegaire) whom St Patrick challenged.

The Anglo-Norman invasion forced a Corca Laoidhe sept to move west into Inchigeela. There they became under-chiefs to the Muskerry MacCarthys.

Writings of John O'Leary (1830–1907) assisted the Fenian movement. Editor of the *Irish People*, he was convicted for treason and imprisoned in 1865. After subsequent exile, he returned. He described Maude Gonne as a 'rabble rouser', yet heroicised her in 'No Second Troy'. An early exponent of 'working a crowd', he once told W.B. Yeats: 'There are things a man must not do to save a nation.' When Yeats asked what, O'Leary replied 'Cry in public'. He encouraged and influenced the young Yeats, who later wrote in 'September 1913':

> Romantic Ireland's dead and gone
> It's with O'Leary in the grave.

On 8 October 1871 a fire occurred in the barn of Patrick and Catherine O'Leary, 137 De Koven Street, Chicago, when a cow kicked over a bucket. The blaze spread through the city's wooden structures. The 'Great Fire of Chicago' claimed 300 lives and destroyed 17,500 buildings, leaving 100,000 people homeless.

An tAthair Peadar Ó Laoghaire (1839–1920) embraced Land War politics. He wrote Irish as he heard it spoken in classics like *Séadna* (telling of a shoemaker's struggle with the Devil) and *Mo Scéal Féin*. He translated the Gospels and *The Imitation of Christ*.

At Givenchy, France, in 1915, Lance Corporal Mick O'Leary of the 1st Irish Guards captured enemy barricades almost single-handedly. He received the Victoria Cross and recruiting posters carried his picture.

More recently

One Michael O'Leary was Minister for Labour and leader of the Labour Party, while another Michael O'Leary, Managing Director of Ryanair, pioneered low-fare flying from Ireland.

And 'One, two, three O'Leary' was a popular children's skipping game.

O'NEILL
Neal, *Neill*, Nihill, O'Neal, Ó Neighill, Ó Néill, O'Nihill

Motto: Lamh Dearg Éirinn (The Red Hand of Ireland)

The name derives from the Norse Njall. In Irish, it became Niall. Niall of the Nine Hostages was progenitor of the formidable O'Neills of Tyrone.

Conn O'Neill (*c.* 1484–1559) was First Earl of Tyrone. His son Shane (1530–67) was known as Seán an Díomais or Shane the Proud. Having persuaded Queen Elizabeth I to accept his territorial rights, he plundered lands of other chieftains, attacked the Pale and sacked Armagh. After losing to Sir Hugh O'Donnell at Lough Swilly (1567), he sought asylum with the

McDonnells at Cushendun, County Antrim. Remembering his earlier assaults on them, they murdered him.

Sir Phelim O'Neill (1604–53) was a philanderer who drew down loans on the strength of his extensive Ulster territories. MP for Dungannon in the Irish Parliament of 1641, he participated in the rebellion of that year. As Commander-in-Chief of the Irish forces in Ulster he falsely offered friends commissions as officers on behalf of the King and was executed for treason.

Hugh O'Neill, Third Baron of Dungannon and Second Earl of Tyrone (1550–1616), led a tempestuous personal and public life. His four marriages had more to do with annexing property than with romance. Protracted disputes and warfare, mainly to recover lost estates, culminated in the Battle of the Yellow Ford, near Armagh (1598). A convincing victory earned him the soubriquet 'Prince of Ireland'. Strong armies from England failed to quash him. In 1601, he joined Red Hugh O'Donnell and moved south to join up with the Spanish expected at Kinsale. Confusion led to an unlikely defeat that initiated the termination of the Gaelic order. Eventually, he lost all his lands and joined 'The Flight of the Earls'.

Owen Roe O'Neill (c. 1590–1649) was Hugh's nephew. He received military experience in Spain before sailing to continue Ulster's fight against English domination. His defeat of General Munro at the Battle of Benburb (1646) was a historical landmark.

The Clandeboy O'Neill (*Clan Aoidh Bhuidhe*: Yellow Hugh's Clan) was a fourteenth-century County Antrim sept. Branches occupied lands in Thomond, Decies and Ossory.

The Monaghan-born Fenian General John O'Neill (1834–78) founded O'Neill, the county seat and frontier town of Holt County, Nebraska. He led a number of cross-border raids against British military posts in Canada between 1866 and 1871, notably at Fort Erie and Fort Ridgeway.

Flute player Francis O'Neill (1849–1936) from Tralibane, Bantry, County Cork, emigrated and became a shepherd, teacher, sailor and General Superintendent of Police in Chicago. His work *The Music of Ireland* (1903) is the largest collection of dance music ever published.

More recently

Captain Terence O'Neill (1914–90) was Prime Minister of Northern Ireland from 1963 to 1969. His invitation to An Taoiseach, Seán Lemass, to take tea at Stormont in January 1965 was a courageous ground-breaking gesture.

The plays of Eugene O'Neill (1888–1953), son of actor James, are classics. He won the Nobel Prize for Literature in 1936. Among his most famous works are *Desire under the Elms, Long Day's Journey into Night* and *Mourning Becomes Electra*.

Máire O'Neill was the stage name of Molly

Allgood (1887–1952), sister of the celebrated Sarah.

'Tip' (Thomas P.) O'Neill (1912–94) was Speaker of the US House of Representatives and a tireless supporter of Ireland's welfare.

O'SHEA
Ó Sé, Ó Séaghdha, O'Shee, Shay, *Shea*, Shee

Motto: Vincit veritas (Truth conquers)

Seabhac means a 'hawk'. *Seagh* means 'valour' or 'strength'. *Séaghainn* means 'noble' or 'stately'. Genealogists have considered the three roots, but all families are descended from an Iveragh sept, Ó Séaghdha. Branches moved east to Tipperary and Kilkenny in the thirteenth century and Shee became the only Gaelic-Irish name among the Tribes of Kilkenny.

In 1582, Sir Richard Shee established an almshouse in Kilkenny for six 'honest, poor, unmarried men' and six widows past fifty years of age. Perhaps he was an old romantic at heart!

The painter Sir Martin Archer Shee (1769–1850) painted portraits of William Robert Fitzgerald, Second Duke of Leinster, and of Thomas Moore. He secured its charter for the Royal Hibernian Academy.

Kitty O'Shea (1845–1921) was mistress and later wife of Charles Stewart Parnell. Her husband,

Captain William, became MP for Clare and Parnell advanced his career but he filed a petition for divorce from Kitty for her adultery with Parnell. Granted *decree nisi*, the action ruined Parnell.

Two writers in Irish were named Pádraig Ó Séaghdha and used pseudonyms. Conán Maol (Bald Conal, 1855–1928) and Gruagach an Tobair (Warrior or Goblin of the Well, 1864–1927) wrote books and plays.

More recently

Seán Ó Sé, a schoolteacher from Bantry, County Cork, sang with Seán Ó Riada's Ceoltóirí Cualann before pursuing a successful solo career.

Páidi Ó Sé and Jack O'Shea were members of the Kerry Gaelic football teams of the 1970s and 1980s, winning, respectively, eight and seven senior all-Ireland medals.

Milo O'Shea performed in the Pike Theatre and married actress Maureen Toal before leaving Ireland to star on Broadway and in films. He returned to play opposite David Kelly in *Rough for Theatre I* in the *Beckett on Film* television series (2001).

REILLY
Ó Raghailligh, O'Rahilly, Ó Rathaille, O'Reilly, Reily, Rieley, Rielly, Riley, Rilly, Ryely, Ryley

Motto: Dum Spiro Spero (While I breathe, I hope)

Rátháil means 'collector of tithes' but most commentators deny any connection, accepting that Reillys simply were descendants of a warrior of Brian Boru's whose personal name was Raghallach. The Breffny O'Reilly territories extended into Monaghan and later into Leinster, particularly Longford, Meath and Westmeath. Giolla Íosa (Attendant of Jesus) Ó Raghaille founded Cavan's Franciscan monastery (*c.* 1300). It had forty abbots of the name. In the fifteenth century the sept had its own coinage, each piece called a 'Reilly'.

In a poem whose opening words form its title the poet Aodhgán Ó Rathaille (1670–1728) began:

> *Is fada liom oíche fhirfhluich gan suan, gan srann*
> Long is the soaking night, without peace,
>   without snore.

He and The O'Rahilly (1875–1916), 1916 Rebellion victim, were of another distinct sept.

Edward O'Reilly (*c.* 1769–1829) compiled the first English–Irish dictionary.

A close associate of the patriot John Mitchel, Thomas Devin Reilly (1824–54) helped edit *The Nation*. Later, he edited the *Democratic Review* (New York) and the *Washington Union*.

Myles O'Reilly (1835–80) was Officer Commanding the Irish Brigade in the Papal Service. Five O'Reillys were archbishops of Armagh; another five bishops of Kilmore. Two were Clogher bishops and one ruled the diocese of Derry. During the eighteenth century, Count Don

Alexander O'Reilly, after military service as a high-ranking officer in French, Austrian and Spanish armies, became Governor of Louisiana.

More recently

In sport, 'The Gallant John Joe' O'Reilly was captain of the Cavan Gaelic football team. He received the Sam Maguire Cup at the Polo Grounds, New York, in 1947 and the following year in Croke Park, Dublin.

Brendan O'Reilly (1929–2001) was an athlete, singer and sports commentator who had a passionate interest in the life of Michael Collins.

Tony (Sir Anthony) O'Reilly's distinction in rugby became overshadowed by his success as an international entrepreneur.

The fictitious comes to the fore yet again, so let us end with a rousing chorus!

Come back, Paddy Reilly, to Ballyjamesduff
Come home, Paddy Reilly, to me.

RYAN
Mulryan, Ó Maoilriain, Ó Riain, O'Ryan, Royan, *Ruane*

Motto: Malo mori quam foedari (I would rather die than be disgraced)

Considerable argument has failed to resolve the origin of the basic *riain* common to all forms of the name Ryan. From the Latin *rîtus* through the Irish, it would suggest one who assembles in order or who marshals or sets a course. *Rian* is a 'path' or 'course' while *fear cinn riain* is a 'pacemaker' or 'leader'. Most scholars have dismissed an archaic Irish word for water with similar spelling.

The name is now most common in County Tipperary, many of whose hurlers have borne the name with distinction. That county's border with Limerick was straddled by a barony once called Owney O'Mulryan. Mulryan was then by far the most common form but not any more.

Separately, the Ó Riains formed a minor Leinster sept descended from Cathaoir Mór, a second-century king of the province. Its chief was lord of Uí Drone in County Carlow and the name is still strong in that county.

Eamonn an Cnoic, or Ned of the Hill, the subject of a celebrated poem, was a Tipperary rapparee. Formally, he was Edward Ryan (1680–1724) from Knockmell and tradition claims he wrote the poem himself:

> Oh, dark is the evening, and silent the hour.
> Who is the minstrel by yonder lone tower?
> His harp all so tenderly touching with skill
> Oh, who can it be but young Ned of the Hill?

The Ryans of Tomcoole, County Wexford, were a political family, of whom Phyllis married Seán T. Ó Ceallaigh (see Kelly). One of them, Dr James Ryan (1891–1970), was a medical officer for the 1916 Rebellion, a TD, a founder member of Fianna Fáil and Minister for Finance.

Republican and socialist Frank Ryan (1902–44) led a 200-strong contingent to fight with the International Brigade against General Franco in the Spanish Civil War.

Some Irish Ryans became American clerics of note. Patrick J. was Archbishop of Philadelphia. Abram was an American Civil War poet and chaplain for the Confederate Army; he wrote 'The Sword of Robert E. Lee' and 'Reunited, Erin's Flag'. Stephen was Bishop of Buffalo.

Thomas 'Fortune' Ryan (1851–1928) became a millionaire through insurance trading in the US. He had his supporters, but businessman Thomas W. Lawson used the terms 'Muckraker' and 'Bucket Shop Shark' in repudiating him and other figures of the 'Roaring Twenties'. He had Mexican-Indian and Mexican-Irish parents.

Representing the US, Limerick man Paddy Ryan (1882–1964) won the hammer event at the Olympic Games in Antwerp in 1920.

More recently

Two Ryans wrote extensively about wars. Desmond (1893–1964), who was secretary to Padraic Pearse, concerned himself with Irish conflicts, and Cornelius (1920–74) covered campaigns and leaders in World War Two. *The Longest Day* is his most celebrated work.

Tony Ryan became a giant in modern Irish aviation and the airline Ryanair pioneered economy fares.

Again, however, one of the most celebrated bearers of the name was fictitious – *Ryan's Daughter*.

SMITH

Goan, Gow, *Gowan*, McCona, Mac Gabhann, McGough, MacGowan, *McGowan*, Magough, Ó Gabhan, O'Gowan, *Smyth*

Motto: Luceo non uro (I shine but do not burn)

The most common name in England, Scotland and Wales comes fifth in Ireland. Yet it is not always Anglo-Irish, since the Irish *gabhann* is the genetive of *gabha*, meaning a 'smith' or 'blacksmith'. This patronymic altered to MacGowan, Cleary and Clarke. Griffith's Valuation of Ireland (1848–64) shows Smiths and Smyths in almost every Irish county. While many of them bear personal names suggesting British origins, the number of Patrick Smiths is staggering, particularly in the Cavan–Monaghan–Louth–Down area. Obviously, holders of the Irish variants often were smiths by trade.

Waterford-born Charles Smith (*c.* 1715–62) pioneered Irish topography and wrote a series of county and city histories.

Dubliner Henry John S. Smith (1826–83) was a celebrated mathematician at Oxford. He was an authority on the theory of numbers, geometry and elliptic functions.

At the age of nine, James Smith (*c.* 1720–1806) emigrated from Dublin to the US with his father.

In Pennsylvania, he became an iron-master and lawyer and was a friend and supporter of George Washington. He was a signatory of the American Declaration of Independence.

William Smyth (1813–78) of Dublin was a British navy midshipman before becoming Public Treasurer of Dublin. An actor, painter and writer, he befriended William Makepeace Thackeray and 'Father Prout' (see Mahony).

More recently

Rosemary Smith won a variety of motor rallying and racing events at home and abroad. She was the first Irish woman to win an international event outright while competing against men.

Michelle Smith (de Bruin) won three gold medals and one bronze at the 1996 Olympic Games in Atlanta, Georgia.

Shane MacGowan of The Pogues and later The Popes was born in England while his Irish parents were on vacation there.

STEWART

le Steward, Mac Stíobhard, Steuart, Steward, *Stuart*

Motto: Audaces fortuna juvat (Fortune favours the bold)

Obviously of Scottish origin, all forms are found mostly in Ulster, yet Stewart is still one of the most common non-indigenous names in Ireland. Le Steward is an Anglo-Norman form. *Stiobhard* is a direct translation of the word 'steward' and has no indigenous status. Roman Catholics were inclined towards the Stuart spelling.

In 1760, John Stuart Moore built Stuart Hall, seat of Lord Castlestewart. It is situated three miles from Stewartstown, County Tyrone. Sir Alexander Stewart also built a castle near the town.

Dublin's Stewart's Hospital was originally Palmerstown House. John Hely-Hutchinson (see Healy) built it in 1763. Later it bore the abominable name The Stewart Institution for Idiotic and Imbecile Children.

Dublin-born Robert Stewart, Viscount Castlereagh (1769–1822), was Chief Secretary during the 1798 Rebellion. He secured the passage of the Act of Union (1800). He was later Secretary of War and Foreign Secretary. A number of controversial repressive policies in which he figured affected him and he committed suicide.

Dublin Castle's Chapel Royal (built 1807–14), St Werburgh's and Great St George's churches have woodcarvings by Richard Stewart. Interestingly, in 1957, artist Alastair Stewart restored the paintings in the Castle's State Apartments.

Charles Stewart Parnell's mother, Delia, was the daughter of a famous US naval hero, Commodore Charles Stewart.

More recently

Jackie Stewart was one of the most successful Grand Prix racing drivers. He won the event twenty-seven times before he retired in 1973.

Controversial poet and writer Francis Stuart (1902–2000) won the patronage of W.B. Yeats. He endured accusations of assisting German propaganda during World War Two. In his later years, he became a saoí of Aosdána.

And how could we neglect film star James Stewart? Aw naw!

SULLIVAN
Ó Súilleabháin, Ó Súillobháin, *O'Sullivan*, Shorelahan, Soolivan, *Soraghan*, Sulavan, Sulevan, Sulivan, Sullavan, Sullevan

Motto: Lámh foisteanach abú (Steady hand forever)

The most obvious translation of the name, 'one eye', is often disputed. *Súil* is certainly 'eye', but the second and third syllables might have emerged from *bán*, so 'white eyed' (albino) or the 'eye (keeper) of the plain' must receive consideration. The third most common name in all Ireland becomes first in Munster, particularly in Counties Cork and Kerry and, to a lesser extent, in County Limerick.

Eoghan Mór (Big Eoin) was father of Oilioll Olum, from whom sprang many leading Munster families. One of these, the O'Sullivans, had lands in County Tipperary but the Anglo-Norman invasion pushed them south-west. A number of sub-sects emerged, the most important being O'Sullivan Mór (Kenmare area of Kerry) and O'Sullivan Beare (Beare peninsula, Cork). The latter's keep at Dunboy, near Castletown Bearhaven, was the last fortification in the south-west to fall to the forces of Elizabeth I in the Nine Years War. Dónal Cam (Bent) O'Sullivan Beare (1560–1618) withstood Sir George Carew's fierce assault for a week. He escaped the hanging and carnage that ensued by retreating to Glengarriff. Sir Charles Wilmot defeated him there and Dónal set out on an incredible two-week march to Leitrim. He arrived at the O'Rourke's castle near Dromahaire on 14 January 1603 with just thirty-five of his 1,000-strong army.

The poet Eoghan Ruadh Ó Súilleabháin was born in Kerry in 1748. Often called the 'Irish Robert Burns' or Eoghan an Bhéil Bhinn (Eoin of the Sweet Mouth), he died in 1784 as a result of a brawl. The poem upon which he was working when drawing close to death went:

> *Sin é an file go fann*
> *Nuair thuiteann an peann as a láimh.*

> That is the feeble poet
> When the pen falls from his hand.

T.D. Sullivan (1827–1914) from Bantry, County Cork, published his song 'God Save

Ireland' in *The Nation*. Before the Battle of Fredericksburg in the American Civil War (1862) Irish men among the Northern troops began toasting 'Old Dairt' ('Old Clod', their version of 'Old Sod', Ireland) and singing his 'Song of the Canadian Backwoods'. Southern troops heard them and joined in. For almost thirty minutes, the misty hills echoed to the voices:

> Ireland Boys, Hooray! Ireland Boys, Hooray!
> We'll toast old Ireland, dear old Ireland
> Ireland Boys, Hurrah!

Spirited folklore evolved around Sergeant Michael Sullivan of the 24th Georgia Regiment for heroic actions at the Battle of Fredericksburg.

The 'Boston Strong Boy' John L. Sullivan was world heavyweight boxing champion from 1882 to 1892. His father was from Tralee, County Kerry, and his mother from Athlone, County Westmeath.

Sir Arthur Seymour Sullivan (1842–1900) was a composer of light operas of which William Gilbert was lyricist. Apart from the popular Gilbert and Sullivan works, he composed 'Onward, Christian Soldiers' and 'The Lost Chord'.

More recently

Pilgrims visit the shrine of the Jesuit priest, Fr John Sullivan (1861–1933), in St Francis Xavier's Church, Gardiner Street, Dublin. A postulator for his beatification and canonisation was appointed in 1947.

Dublin-born artist Seán O'Sullivan (1906–64) painted W.B. Yeats, James Joyce and Eamon de Valera among others.

Two O'Sullivans became Chiefs of Staff of the Irish army, Carl (1976–78) and Gerald (1984–86).

World champion athlete Sonia O'Sullivan won a silver medal at the 2000 Olympics in Sydney.

SWEENEY

Mac Suibhne, Mac Suichne, MacSweeny, McSweeny, McSwiney, Sweeny, Swiney

No motto

Mac Suibhne is also the Irish form of Swayne but most chronologists believe Swayne to be a synonym of Swan. *Suibhne* is the antonym of *duibhne* (meaning 'unpleasant'). It was an early Irish personal name. St Suibhne is associated with the Skelligs off the Kerry coast. In the seventh century, an abbot of Cork and a high king were named, respectively, Suibhne Mac Máele and Suibhne Menn. Folklore tells how St Ronan cursed a Suibhne and the unfortunate man went insane during the Battle of Moira, County Down (637). Thinking he was a bird, he went dashing about woods and thickets. He became known as 'Mad Sweeney'.

There was a St Suibhne in Iona, Scotland, and many galloglass settlers in Donegal were from that country. Donegal septs included 'MacSweeney the Battleaxes' and the MacSweeneys of Banagh and of Fanad. The name spread mainly to Munster, where a branch fought for the MacCarthys of Muskerry.

Playwright and producer Owen MacSwiney (*c.* 1675–1754) managed Drury Lane Theatre and the Queen's Theatre, London. King George II appointed him Keeper of the King's Mews. He willed his considerable wealth to the Dublin actress Peg Woffington (1714–60).

Terence MacSwiney (1879–1920), author, playwright and revolutionary, was a founder member of the Cork Celtic Literary Society and Cork Dramatic Society. As a TD in the First Dáil he helped establish its Arbitration Courts. Succeeding the murdered Tomás Mac Curtain as Lord Mayor of Cork, he was arrested and imprisoned in Brixton. He endured forced feeding during his hunger strike and died after seventy-four days. In 1919, his sister, Mary (1872–1942), testified in Washington on conditions in Ireland. Aggressively anti-Treaty, she was imprisoned during the Irish Civil War and continued to reject the legitimacy of the southern state until her death.

More recently

Concert pianist Veronica Mary McSwiney went on world tours. She recorded 'John Field Nocturnes' and other works. In later years she encouraged and trained young musicians and singers.

The group 'Sweeney's Men' lasted only from 1966 to 1969, yet had a revolutionary effect on the Celtic folk music revival.

And beware Sweeney Todd, the Demon Barber of Fleet Street!

WALSH
Branagh, Brannagh, *Brannick*, Brawnick, Brennagh, O'Brannagh, Ó Breathnach, Ó Breatnach, *Wallace*, Wallsh, Walshe, Welch, Welsh

Motto: Meliora spero (I hope for better things)

The Irish *Breatnach* means a person from Wales and the name occurs most often in Counties Mayo, Kilkenny, Waterford, Galway and Cork. The fourth most common name in Ireland is Cambro-Norman. An early twelfth-century invader, Philip the Welshman, came to the south-east shore with his brother David and son Haylen. Issue from these Breatnachs and from others who followed formed septs that included landowners of Castlehowel (Kilkenny), Ballyrichmore (Waterford) and Ballykileavan (Laois). Settlers in an area enveloping a small mountain ridge in Kilkenny earned it the name Walsh (or Welsh) Mountains. Others spread around the southern shore, with a few filtering up the west coast also. Most of the settlers became establishment figures in the judiciary and the army but some chose to support the native Irish in the Nine Years War.

A study of the Walshes of Tirawley in Mayo claims that they stem from a Welshman named Walynus.

The form Welsh simply described people from Wales or may also have evolved through the pronunciation of the root form (pronounced 'Wawlsh') in a southern accent.

People of note bearing one form of the name are numerous. Many eminent churchmen were Walshs. The County Kildare-born Franciscan Peter Walsh (*c.* 1614–88) defended the royalist cause in the civil wars of 1642–49. After the Restoration (1660), he published works promoting loyalty to the restored English monarchy. These included *The History and Vindication of the Loyal Formulary of Irish Remonstrance* (1674).

Two Walshs, Robert (1772–1852) and Richard Hussey (1825–62), wrote extensively on metallic currency, medals and gems.

Edward Walsh (1805–50) contributed nationalist poems to George Petrie's *Dublin Penny Journal* and Michael Walsh (1897–1938) was the 'Poet of Fore' in County Westmeath.

Kerry's Maurice Walsh (1879–1964) wrote celebrated works like *The Key Above the Door*, *The Small Dark Man* and *Blackcock's Feather* but is now best known for his short story that became a film, *The Quiet Man*.

During the Irish War of Independence an alleged decoy to allow IRA men on the run escape

from Templemore, County Tipperary, involved
'Bleeding Statues' in the home of a Walsh family.
Crowds attracted by the 'phenomenon' facilitated
escape.

More recently

Joe Walsh was a pioneer in holiday tour operations
abroad.

'Builder' Walsh was a celebrated Kilkenny
hurler and Ted Walsh was a champion jockey
before turning his hand to training horses,
including Istabraque.

WHITE

**Banane, Bane, Baun, Bawn,
de Faoite, *Galligan*, Kilbane,
Whight, *Whyte***

Motto: The noblest motive is the public good

This English name widely and frequently found in
Ireland has been accorded the translation de Faoite.
Bán is the true Irish for 'white' and *geal* is 'bright',
so the synonyms represent usages of these words.
Some scholars consider Whitty, MacWhitty and
McQuitty as synonyms but most agree that they
are from a separate MacWhite origin.

Settlers in Limerick and Clare held,
respectively, municipal office and property.

In 1738, Fr James White published a history of
Limerick.

Poet Samuel Whyte (1733–1811) taught Arthur Wellesley, who became the First Duke of Wellington. The young Richard Brinsley Sheridan and Thomas Moore attended his Dublin school also.

Field Marshal Sir George Stuart White VC, OM (1835–1912) from Antrim served in Burma and became Military Secretary, Viceroy and Commander-in-Chief in India. He was besieged in Ladysmith during the Boer War. Later, he became Governor of Gibraltar, then Governor of Chelsea Hospital. His son, Captain James Robert (Jack, 1879–1946) DSO, became his aide-de-camp. Jack later supported Roger Casement, James Larkin and James Connolly and was organiser of the Irish Citizen Army and, in Derry and Tyrone, the Irish Volunteers. Dismissed from the British army for advocating acceptance of the Volunteers as an Irish defence force, he served in an ambulance unit in France for two years of the Great War.

More recently

'Boiler' White was a 'Lilywhite' – a Kildare footballer of note in the 1940–50s.

Novelist, playwright and journalist William John (Jack) White (1920–80) became Controller of Television Programmes and later Head of Resources in RTÉ.

Author and critic Terence de Vere White (1912–94) was Literary Editor of *The Irish Times*

(1963–78). He wrote biographies of Kevin O'Higgins and Isaac Butt and a study of *The Parents of Oscar Wilde and Tom Moore*.

James White, Director of the National Gallery of Ireland (1964–80), was an art critic of note. By their unpretentious style, his lectures and writings helped to make art accessible and non-elitist.

WILSON
Willison, Willson

Motto: Res, non verba (Action, not words)

The twenty-sixth most common name in Ireland is the country's most common British name. It originated in Scotland and England and spread, mainly to Ulster.

William Edward Wilson (1851–1908), High Sheriff of County Westmeath, was an astronomer and physicist of note. He pioneered study of the sun's temperature and radiation in sunspots.

Kilkenny man Denys Corbett Wilson made the first plane flight from Britain (Fishguard) to Ireland. He landed his Bleriot XI at Crane, County Wexford, on 22 April 1912.

Thomas Woodrow Wilson (1856–1924) was President of the US from 1913 to 1921. His grandfather, James, was from Strabane and his grandmother was Amy Adams from Sion Mills, both in County Tyrone.

At Currygrane, County Longford, Seán Mac Eoin, the 'Blacksmith of Ballinalee', shod horses for Sir Henry Wilson (1864–1922). Having fought in the Boer War and in Burma, Wilson held prestigious appointments in the British army, reaching Chief of the Imperial Staff in February 1918 with the rank of Field Marshal. A close associate of Lloyd George, he supported Ulster unionists and exhorted oppressive measures in Ireland. After his army service, he became MP for North Down and continued pursuing anti-nationalist policies. He was shot dead outside his London home in June 1922.

From Blackrock, County Dublin, engineer Walter Gordon Wilson (1874–1957) designed the Wilson Pilcher and Armstrong Whitworth motor cars. The Hallford lorry was among his other mechanical innovations.

More recently

American friend of Noel Coward's, John Chapman Wilson (1899–1961) was a theatre and musical director and producer. His fellow countrymen August and Lanford Eugene Wilson were influential playwrights.

James Harold Wilson (1916–95) was twice British Prime Minister (1964–70 and 1974–76).

Actor and director Georges Wilson directed the Theatre National Populaire in Paris from 1963 to 1972.

Marie Wilson lost her life in the Enniskillen

bombing atrocity of 1987 as she held the hand of her father, Gordon Wilson (1927–95). He moved many hearts by his forgiving attitude and he became a member of Seanad Éireann.

GLOSSARY

Act of Union: The British and Irish parliaments passed two similar measures in 1800 to create the United Kingdom of Great Britain and Ireland. The resulting Act of Union came into force on 1 January 1801.

Aileach: The territory that, in the main, is now County Donegal. 'The Grianán of Aileach', the Northern Uí Néill seat, was a fortified site on Greenan Mountain in Donegal. It was destroyed in 1101 by Muiriertach O'Brien, King of Munster, in revenge for the destruction of Kincora (see MacLoughlin).

Anglo-Norman invasion: The original Normans were from Normandy in northern France. They conquered England in 1066. Those who invaded Ireland were mainly Welsh settlers (Cambro-Normans). As mercenaries, they accompanied the exiled King of Leinster, Dermot MacMurrough, in his 1167 repatriation. Other invaders, including Strongbow, followed (1169–72). This resulted in the involvement of England in Irish affairs because of English fears that the Norman settlers might set up a rival dynasty in Ireland.

annals: A number of annals chronicle Irish affairs over certain periods. Those referred to are Innisfallen (eleventh to fourteenth centuries), The Four Masters (Annales Rioghachta Éireann – Annals of the Kingdom of Ireland, 1632–36), Tighernach (late eleventh century, but this is disputed), Loch Cé (1014–1590), Connaught (Annála Connacht, 1224–1554) and Ulster (fifteenth to seventeenth centuries).

Annaly: An ancient territory embracing the complete county of Longford and portions of Counties Westmeath and Leitrim.

Aosdána: (People of art) Taken from an old Irish term for practitioners in trades, arts, crafts and professions and applied in 1983 to an Irish Arts Council

affiliation of artists selected for receipt of state
pensions (see *saoi* below).

barony: A sub-division of a county.

Battle of Benburb: In County Tyrone, on
5 June 1646, Owen Roe O'Neill (Confederate
Catholics) beat the Scottish army under Robert
Munro who were defending the Ulster planters.

Battle of Kinsale: (24 December 1601) A Spanish
expeditionary force landed at Kinsale but was
contained by Lord Mountjoy. Mountjoy then routed
Hugh O'Neill (Earl of Tyrone) and Red Hugh
O'Donnell who had marched south to assist the
Spanish. The Spanish then withdrew.

black rent: Protection money raised by Gaelic lords
from tenants and sometimes from the Dublin
government.

Book of Armagh: Contains the Confessions of St
Patrick, a copy of the New Testament and lives of
saints including St Martin of Tours, all compiled by
Feardomhnach the Scribe *c.* 807.

Book of Ballymote: Contains an Irish version of Virgil's
Aeneid, the Ogham alphabet, a copy of the Book
of Rights and other material compiled by Maghnus
Ó Duibhgeannáin and others *c.* 1390.

Breffny: The territory that is now Counties Cavan and
Leitrim. Also spelt Breifne, Breiffiny, Breifny and
Breny.

Brehon Law or System: The legal system that existed
prior to the Anglo-Norman invasion (see above).
Breitheamh means judge.

Brian Boru: (*c.* 941–1014) 'Brian of the [Cattle]
Tributes' was so called because of his exacting them
from the O'Neills. He was King of Dál gCais (see
below) and later High King of Ireland. He is
renowned for defeating the Leinster men and their
Norse allies at the Battle of Clontarf (Dublin) in 1014
before being killed by a fleeing enemy.

Cambro-Norman: See *Anglo-Norman invasion* above.

Carbery: A region around the present town of Ross Carbery, County Cork, that, in the twelfth century, was owned by the lords of Carbery.

cenél: (cineál) Race or descendants.

Cenél Conaill: Donegal (Tirchonaill) descendants of Conall Gulban, a son of Niall of the Nine Hostages (see below).

Cenél Eachrach: An Ulster population group.

Cenél Eoghan: Tyrone and Derry descendants of Eoghan, a son of Niall of the Nine Hostages (see below), i.e. O'Neills.

clan: A Scottish group with common ancestors, particularly Highlanders under patriarchal control. There was no Irish clan system.

co-arb: See *erenagh* below.

cognate: Descended from a common ancestor.

Connello: A Limerick barony (Upper or Lower).

Corcabaskin: A region in what is now west County Clare.

Corca Laoidhe: A region in what is now south-west County Cork.

Corcomroe: A coastal barony in the north of what is now County Clare.

Cumann na mBan: A women's organisation founded in 1913 that became a division of the Irish Volunteers.

Dáil Éireann: The lower house of the Irish parliament, commonly referred to as the Dáil.

dál: A region.

Dalcassian: See *Dál gCais* below.

Dál Fiatach: A region in the east of the present County Down.

Dál gCais: A region occupied by Dalcassians who constituted the main septs of Thomond (see below). The Dalcassians belonged to the Uí Toirdealbhaigh sept and only gained prominence in Thomond through the greatness of Brian Boru (see above; also see *Eoghanacht* below).

Dál nAraidi: A region around Lough Neagh.

Dál Ríada: A region in the north of the present County Antrim.

Decies: A region in the west of the present County Waterford.

Dermot MacMurrough: (Diarmuid Mac Murchadha, 1110–71) A King of Leinster who was the primary cause of the Anglo-Norman invasion (see above).

Desmond: South Munster territory comprising all of the present County Kerry and much of County Cork (see *Eoghanacht* below).

donn: Brown.

EEC: European Economic Community.

Eoghanacht: In the third century, a Munster king, Oilioll Olum, had sons Eoghan and Cormac Cas. When he died, Cormac Cas inherited Thomond (see below and *Dál gCais* above). Eoghan received the territory of Desmond (see above). His family were known as the Eoghanacht.

eponymous ancestor: The person from whom a family name originated.

erenagh: The *aircinnech* (erenagh) or lay head of a church. Church property was handed down to his family. An ordained head or abbot was called co-arb (*comarba*: heir).

Fenian Dynamiters: A triumvirate with the nickname 'The Triangle' that conducted a dynamiting campaign in England during the 1880s.

Fenians: A republican movement formally founded during 1858 by John O'Mahony in New York and James Stephens in Dublin.

fionn: Fair.

'Flight of the Earls': A romantic term for the self-imposed exile in 1607 of Rory O'Donnell, Earl of Tirchonaill, Hugh O'Neill, Earl of Tyrone, Cúconnacht Maguire, Lord of Fermanagh, and their followers.

Foherta: Forth (see below).

Forth: A small barony in County Carlow and a larger one in County Wexford.

Four Tribes of Tara: From County Meath, the Connollys, O'Harts, O'Kellys and O'Regans spread to County Laois and other midland territories.

Gaelic: (a) The language spoken in the Scottish highlands. (b) An adjective denoting the race inhabiting Ireland since the prehistoric era. (c) The language known in English as the Irish language now spelt Gaeilge in that tongue.

galloglass: (*gall óglac*: foreign warrior) Paid fighting man retained permanently as such by an Irish chieftain. They were mainly from Innse Gall in the Hebrides (Scotland) and were heavily armed, while the kern (*ceithearn*: war band) were lightly armed.

Geraldine: (Gearaltach) A term used to describe the Fitzgerald family, medieval earls of Desmond and of Kildare. They and other English families were rebels who regarded themselves as gentlemen of blood and who became accomplices of the Irish.

Iar Connacht: A region, mainly in west Connaught, now known as Connemara.

IRB: Irish Republican Brotherhood. A secret organisation that emerged from the Fenian movement (see above).

Iregan: (Uí Riagáin) A region of ancient Ophaley now in the north-west Slieve Bloom Mountains of County Laois. The Ó Duinn (see Dunne) ruled there. Anglicised also to Dooregan, Duoregan, Hyregan, Oregan and Yregan.

Irish Volunteers: A southern nationalist force founded in November 1913.

Iveragh: A barony in south-west County Kerry.

kern: See *galloglass* above.

Kincora: Seat of Dalcassian and Thomond kings at Killaloe, County Clare.

Mac: A prefix meaning 'son of', often abbreviated to Mc (see Introduction).

Mag: A form of Mac (see above) used before a vowel, e.g. Mag Uidhir, as in Maguire.

Magunihy: An east County Kerry barony.

Mc: See *Mac* above.

MEP: Member of the European Parliament.

mod.: Modern.

MP: Member of Parliament.

Muskerry: (Muscraidhe) A region in the north-west and centre of the present County Cork.

Muskerylinn: Part of Muskerry between Ballyvourney and Blarney.

Nation, The: A journal founded in 1842 by Thomas Davis, John Blake Dillon and Charles Gavan Duffy. It espoused the establishment of 'internal union and external independence' and strove 'to create and foster public opinion and make it racy of the soil'. It developed into a voice for the Young Ireland movement.

Niall of the Nine Hostages: (Niall Noígiallach) Progenitor of the Uí Néill. Some sources name him as High King of Ireland from 379 to 405, while others place his activities in the fifth and ninth centuries.

Nine Years War: (1593–1603) Also known as 'Tyrone's Rebellion' because the main protagonist was Hugh O'Neill, Second Earl of Tyrone. Elizabethan partition of County Monaghan crippled the MacMahon lordship and threatened similar consequences on other Ulster lordships. Traditional Ulster rivalry dissipated in face of this threat. The long campaign included celebrated battles like Clontibret (1595) and the Yellow Ford (1598). The outcome, after O'Neill's submission at Mellifont in 1603, gave England complete control of Ireland for the first time since the Anglo-Norman invasion (see above).

Normans: See *Anglo-Norman invasion* above.

Ó: (singular) Uí (plural) Literally meaning 'from', i.e. descendant(s) of.

O'Neills of Tyrone: Legendary figures in Ireland's history.

Oriel: (Orghialla). A region comprising the present Counties Monaghan and Armagh and parts of Counties Down (south), Fermanagh and Louth.

Ossory: (Osraighe) A region comprising the present County Kilkenny and parts of adjoining counties.

Owney: Territory that later became incorporated in the County Tipperary barony of Owney and Arra.

Pale, The: An area around County Dublin and extending to parts of Counties Louth, Kildare and Meath (and further, periodically). The 'English Pale' emerged after 1400 as a defensive measure against growing Gaelic Irish threats.

Penal Laws: (or Popery Laws) Statutes introduced from 1695 discriminating against Roman Catholics.

rapparee: (*rapáire*: half pike) A seventeenth-century highwayman who sought to defend peasants from the oppressor or an independent, maverick soldier.

Red Branch Knights: Military guardians of Ulster during the reign of Conchubhar Mac Nessa. Cuchullain was their renowned warrior.

Repealer: Anyone demanding repeal of the Act of Union (see above) and restoration of a separate Irish parliament.

RTÉ: Radio Telefís Éireann, Ireland's national broadcasting service.

rua: Red.

saoí: A rank among members of Aosdána (see above).

Seanad Éireann: The upper house of the Irish parliament.

sept: A collective term describing a group of people who bore a common surname and inhabited a particular area or whose ancestors were known to have occupied that area.

Seven Septs of Laois: Macaboys (i.e. MacEvoys, also The Clandeboys), O'Devoys (or O'Deevys), O'Dorans, O'Dowlings, O'Kellys, O'Lalors and O'Mores.

Síol Anamchadha: A population group that was a branch of the Uí Máine (see below).

Síol Muireadhaigh: A population group that included the O'Connors and other north Connaught septs.

SJ: Society of Jesus, better known as the Jesuits, a Roman Catholic religious order.

Suaithni: Septs who ruled the territory that is now Balrothery West in County Dublin.

Tánaiste: Deputy Taoiseach (see below).

Taoiseach: (Literally Leader, Ruler, Chief) The Prime Minister of the government of Ireland.

TD: (Teachta Dála) Deputy of Dáil Éireann (see above).

Thomond: (*Tuath Mhumhan* or north Munster) A region taking in most of the present County Clare and portions of Counties Tipperary and Limerick bordering it.

Tirawley: A region in the present County Mayo.

Tirchonaill: (Land of Connell) A region covering the present County Donegal.

Tirowen: (Land of Eoghan) A region comprising the present County Tyrone and part of County Derry.

toponymic: A surname that evolved from the name of a place.

Treaty: An agreement between Ireland and Britain signed on 6 December 1921 that gave independence to twenty-six counties of Ireland.

Tribes of Galway: Mainly Norman merchants controlling municipal administration in late medieval Galway. Some sources claim only seven but most recognise fourteen, namely Athy, Blake, Bodkin, Browne, Darcy, Deane, Font, French, Joyce, Kirwan, Lynch, Martin, Morris and Skerret.

Tribes of Kilkenny: Ten families controlling municipal administration in Kilkenny city in 1650. They were: Archdekin, Archer, Cowley, Knaresborough, Langton, Lawless, Lee, Ragget, Rothe and Shee.

Tribes of Tara: See *Four Tribes of Tara* above.

Truce: Cessation of hostilities in the Irish War of Independence that came into effect on 11 July 1921.

Uí: See *Ó* above.

Uí Drone: A population group of the present County Carlow.

Uí Fiachrach: A population group of the present County Sligo and north County Mayo that had a

smaller branch in south County Galway called
Aidhne.

Uí Máine: (sometimes Hy Many) A population group in
the centre of the present County Galway extending
into the south of County Roscommon.

Uí Néill: See *Niall of the Nine Hostages* and *O'Neills of
Tyrone* above.

UN: United Nations.

war cries: Sometimes found in mottoes, Irish battle or
war cries were prohibited by the Establishment. Yet
they survived until the complete conquest of Ireland
by the Stuarts.

Wild Geese: Irish chieftains, their soldiers and followers
who fled to join foreign armies, mainly French, during
the eighteenth century.

Young Irelanders: Followers of a nationalist movement
led by Thomas Davis, Charles Gavan Duffy and John
Blake Dillon (see *Nation, The* above).